Mary Magdalene

Mary Magdalene

The Modern Guide to the Bible's Most Mysterious and Misunderstood Woman

✳

MEERA LESTER

Adams Media
Avon, Massachusetts

Published by Adams Media, an F+W Publications Company
57 Littlefield Street
Avon, MA 02322
www.adamsmedia.com

ISBN: 1-59337-398-8

Printed in Canada.
J I H G F E D C B A

Library of Congress Cataloging-in-Publication Data
Lester, Meera.
Mary Magdalene / by Meera Lester.
p.   cm. Includes bibliographical references.
ISBN 1-59337-398-8
1. Mary Magdalene, Saint I. Title.
BS2485.L47 2005
226'.092--dc22
2005016011

This book is available at quantity discounts for bulk purchases.
For information, please call 1-800-872-5627.

CONTENTS

AUTHOR'S NOTE..XVII

INTRODUCTION... XIX
Who Was Mary Magdalene?.................................... xix
Why Is She So Hotly Debated Today? xxi
How to Use This Book xxi

Part One
A WOMAN FOR ALL TIME ◆ 1

Chapter 1 3

A Much Maligned Mary.. 6
Mary Magdalene's World....................................... 9
The Myth Serves the Church 11
How the Myth Was Made 14
The Gnostics' Portrayal of Mary Magdalene 15
Legends and Scholarly Speculation 17
Ways to Invoke the Holy Blessings of Saint Mary Magdalene....... 20
 Prayer to Saint Mary Magdalene............................ 22

Chapter 2 23

Ambiguity and Supposition 26
Questions about Marriage 29
Mary Magdalene and the Holy Grail 31
The Marriage at Cana.. 36
Mary Magdalene and The Last Supper 39
Speculation about the Beloved Disciple........................ 41
Ways to Invoke the Holy Blessings of Saint Mary Magdalene....... 44
 Prayer to Saint Mary Magdalene............................ 45

Part Two
A WOMAN OF SPIRIT ✦ 47

Chapter 3 49

Gifts of the Holy Spirit.................................... 51
Respected by Others 54
Self-Determined.. 55
Trustworthy 55
Responsible.. 56
Spiritually Evolved....................................... 56
Significance of the Anointing............................... 58
Mary Magdalene's Secret Teaching 61
Ways to Invoke the Holy Blessings of Saint Mary Magdalene....... 62
Reaction from the Apostles 65
     Prayer to Saint Mary Magdalene....................... 68

Chapter 4 69

Mary Belonged in Jesus' World 70
Jesus' Treatment of Women................................ 77
Ways to Invoke the Holy Blessings of Saint Mary Magdalene....... 78
Who Could Be an Apostle?................................. 80
The Thirteenth Apostle 81
Mary's Model for Perfect Leadership 84
Seeds of Discord 84

Marriage or Celibacy?..86
    Prayer to Saint Mary Magdalene...........................89

PART THREE
YOU CAN'T KEEP A GOOD WOMAN DOWN ✦ 91

CHAPTER 5 93

A Power Struggle Ensues..96
Ways to Invoke the Holy Blessings of Saint Mary Magdalene.......98
Tensions Mount...100
Did Mary Magdalene Write the Gospel of John?..................103
Peter's Story Gains Prominence 107
Mary Magdalene Written Out of the Sacred Narrative 109
Medieval Reverence for Mary Magdalene 110
Mary Magdalene's Portrayal in Art 111
The Modern Church Reverses Itself.............................113
    Prayer to Saint Mary Magdalene..........................114

CHAPTER 6 115

Jesus' Pious Widow? 115
Mary's Linkage with Israel's Royal Bloodline 118
The Priory of Sion/Magdalene Connection 119
Mary Magdalene, the Black Madonna, and the Romany 123
The Tarot's Female Pope.......................................126

The Second Eve 127
Pagan Goddess and the Gospel 130
Ways to Invoke the Holy Blessings of Saint Mary Magdalene 132
  Prayer to Saint Mary Magdalene 135

Part Four
MARY MAGDALENE'S WISDOM AND
GUIDANCE FOR TODAY'S WOMAN ✦ 137

Chapter 7 139

Create Holy Space 141
Seek Knowledge from a Sacred Source 143
Cast Out Your Demons 144
Develop Good Spiritual Habits. 149
Take Time-Outs to Reclaim Your Connection to God. 151
Ways to Invoke the Holy Blessings of Saint Mary Madalene 154
Go on a Spiritual Retreat 156
  Novena Prayer to Saint Mary Magdalene 157

Chapter 8 159

Powerful Women, Gentle Warriors 160
Mary's Words Have Modern Resonance 164
Love As Free-Flowing, Sacred Energy 165
Follow Mary's Example of Female Discipleship 167

Make Your Questions Count. 168
Learn to Live an Inner-Directed Life in the World 169
Ways to Invoke the Holy Blessings of Saint Mary Madalene. 170
Be an Advocate for Women Who Desire to Serve. 173
Prayer to Saint Mary Magdalene. 175

PART FIVE
HONORING THE SPIRIT
OF MARY MAGDALENE · 177

CHAPTER 9 179

Invite the Embodiment of Wisdom into Your Life 182
Surround Yourself with Sacred Imagery 187
Open Yourself to the Gifts of Spirit 188
Bring Mary Magdalene into Your Life. 191
Expand Your Network and Build a Spiritual Community. 192
Ways to Invoke the Holy Blessings of Saint Mary Madalene. 194
What Blesses One, Blesses All 197
Prayer to Saint Mary Magdalene. 199

APPENDIX A 201

A Christian Perspective:
An Interview with Reverend Dr. George C. Fitzgerald. 202

A Gnostic Perspective:
An Interview with Rosamonde Miller 206
A Roman Catholic Perspective:
An Interview with Christine Schenk 210

Appendix B 217

    The Surrender 218

Bibliography 219

Sources Quoted/Permissions and Credits 223

Index 225

In memory of her . . .
the woman who knew the All

ACKNOWLEDGMENTS

*B*ehind every book is a visionary. Paula Munier, director of Product Development for Adams Media, conceived the idea and birthed the concept for this book. To her, I owe my deepest gratitude.

I wish to thank Andrea Mattei, my project editor, for her patience, persistence, and ability to coax me back on point when I drifted off course, but especially for being a cheerleader when I needed one.

For her impeccable copyediting skills, consummate professionalism, and unfailing friendship in good times and through rough patches, I am especially grateful to Jan Stiles.

I also wish to thank everyone at Adams Media involved in making this book possible.

I'd like to thank Anita Llewellyn and Kathryn Makris, fellow writers and travelers who share my passion for history, obscure topics, and great stories. Thanks to Gil Garcia for his ardent support.

Finally, I'm especially grateful to my Thursday night writers' group for their brutally honest critiques and loving support. Phyllis, Deb, Cynthia, Dan, Virgil, and Joe, you're the greatest!

AUTHOR'S NOTE

*G*reat effort was made to verify the facts in this work; however, scholars sometimes disagree, and whenever such discrepencies arose in the information describing Mary Magdalene's life, the interpretation of a majority of the sources was the one used in this book.

INTRODUCTION

*M*ary Magdalene was the heroine of one of the Bible's greatest stories, but did you know that she might have been largely edited out of biblical accounts of that story? Speculation runs rampant as to the reasons why. This book examines this and other puzzling mysteries as we journey back into the life and time of this amazing woman.

Who Was Mary Magdalene?

The research and writing of this book invited me to look beyond the Mary Magdalene we know as a religious icon and to see her through the many roles in which she served: devoted follower, friend, leader, and possibly wife (according to one theory). I found her to be a powerful role model and a spiritual example for me and for all women—past, present, and future. The more I read about her, the more intrigued I became, even though there were conflicting accounts, ancient legends, controversial assertions, and minimal references to her in the Bible. Each resource revealed a piece of her story. In writing this book, I have tried to include every interesting morsel and tidbit, both fact and supposition. What emerges is a portrait of Mary Magdalene that may confuse, shock, intrigue, encourage, and challenge its readers.

Mary Magdalene is a sacred sister, someone we can turn to for guidance and support in our modern lives. She lived long ago, but the types of things she had to face are not too different from those that modern women face today. The glass ceiling in corporations as well as the stained-glass ceiling of our churches still exists. Even today, male-dominated cultures keep women in subservient roles, sentenced to a substandard existence with no hope for an education or a better life. Yet, when we look at Mary Magdalene, we can see how a woman who lived in dark times can become a beacon for others. She was a self-actualized person who wasn't afraid to show her loyalty and love when it was dangerous to do so. She neither feared speaking out nor speaking up for others. She claimed her vision, shared her love, walked tall among powerful men, and served as an eloquent spokesperson for Jesus after His death.

In spite of the grief she must have suffered when Jesus was crucified, Mary Magdalene did not despair. She remained on her feet, rushing to finish her work of anointing Jesus' wounded and broken body. Commissioned by the risen Lord to go and tell the other disciples, she searched them out where they had hidden after fleeing in fear of persecution and death. She comforted them. She shared the news that Jesus had risen from the dead. She inspired them with her message. What a strong, powerful woman she must have been.

Why Is She So Hotly Debated Today?

With over seven million copies in print and translations planned for roughly thirty-five languages, the novel *The Da Vinci Code* has single-handedly raised the profile of this mysterious and misunderstood woman who has been biblically marginalized for the last 2,000 years. Women from even the most patriarchal traditions are calling for the recognition of Mary Magdalene and other women of the Bible who traditionally have been misrepresented. Men and women today are forming readers' groups, establishing Web sites, and campaigning for change. Scholars too are contributing commentary and insights into long-hidden and suppressed texts, including the Gospel of Mary Magdalene.

Perhaps, like me, you are ready to expand your knowledge and delve further into the speculation surrounding the life of this amazing but mysterious woman. And perhaps, like me, you will find inspiration and strength in what you learn. This book can further your knowledge about Mary Magdalene and help you understand her more deeply.

How to Use This Book

At the end of this text, check out the bibliography of books and do some further research on Mary Magdalene. View paintings of Mary Magdalene—you'll find many, on the Internet, in books, and in museums all over the world. Bring her blessings of wisdom, goodness, healing, and mercy into your life by doing some or all of the activities listed at the end of each chapter, including prayers, affirmations, meditations, novenas, pilgrimages, and arts-and-crafts projects. Use what you find here as a basis for your own exploration into her life. The journey may lead to many places—to admiration, to strength, to challenges, to devotion to a cause, to penance, to faith, and to peace. Wherever this journey does take you, I hope Mary Magdalene's story is as inspiring for you as it has been for me.

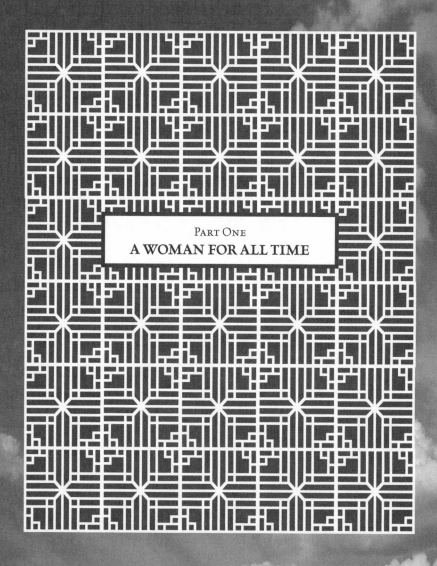

PART ONE

A WOMAN FOR ALL TIME

CHAPTER 1

BEYOND MYTH: Searching for the Truth

*Thou hast turnèd for me my mourning into dancing: thou hast
put off my sackcloth, and girdèd me with gladness.*

—PSALMS 30:11

Mary Magdalene's story is so powerful that, although she lived thousands of years ago, she remains a strong role model for modern women. Imprisoned by the demons of a cursed illness, she had to face life's uncertainties every day—an enduring example of how a woman can become empowered by change. Whether that change subtly shifts us from the status quo or radically redirects us, it always transforms us.

When a life-altering event thrusts our otherwise predictable routines into chaos, many of us feel apprehensive and fear that nothing will ever be the same. Often, a defining moment in our lives launches us into a search for meaning and truth. Maybe the Bible's most mysterious woman—Mary Magdalene—experienced that sort of life-altering event, and perhaps it prompted her to leave the familiarity of her everyday life behind, to embark on a journey with an uncertain future. Whatever her reasons for choosing to make the change, she could not have foreseen the painful and joyous moments to come, and the blessings they would bring.

Those of us who've had to struggle with demons of our own can find hope in Mary Magdalene, the fully human woman. Others who aspire to holiness can take refuge in Mary Magdalene, the saint, the icon. Our modern sisters seek role models for their lives. Who better than Mary Magdalene, whose roles as friend, devoted follower, leader, and even possibly wife (as one theory purports) are found in every culture from ancient to modern time? Her life intrigues us. Why else would so many people study, discuss, and invoke Mary Magdalene—not to mention debate her life so hotly? *The Da Vinci Code*, *The Templar Revelation*, *Holy Blood, Holy Grail*, and other books like them fuel the interest and the controversy. What we really need is a clear lens through which we can fully view Mary Magdalene, a woman for all time.

Mary Magdalene's early life is surrounded by mystery. When she's first mentioned in the Bible, it's in the middle of her personal story. She has chosen to go with the charismatic, itinerant preacher Jesus as He travels around Galilee. Jesus did not call her as He called His twelve chosen disciples. In fact, He didn't call any women the way He asked the males in His entourage to follow Him. But Jesus stands at the center in Mary Magdalene's personal transformation story. Although she is mentioned only fourteen times in the Bible, during the first century her name often appears at the top of the list whenever women's names are mentioned. That is a telling clue—one that seems to suggest her elevated role, one that possibly puts her above others, both men and women, in Jesus' inner circle.

Mary Magdalene is a complex individual who has been portrayed in all sorts of ways. She has been depicted as Jesus' loving companion and trusted confidante. But she has also been characterized as a repentant sinner out of whom Jesus cast seven demons. Healed of her affliction, Mary Magdalene supported Jesus and His followers from her own purse. The position of benefactor or patron suggests yet another important role for Mary Magdalene.

In the Bible, it's clear that Mary Magdalene stood steadfast at Jesus' side during the most significant moments of His life. She was there when Jesus was crucified. After His body was removed from the cross and wrapped in linen for entombment, Mary went to anoint it with spices, unguents, and perfumed oils. But as sundown approached that Friday, Mary was compelled to observe the Jewish Sabbath and was unable to anoint Jesus' body. On Sunday at dawn, she went to Jesus' tomb. There, she became the first person to see the Savior in His transcendent form. It was Mary Magdalene's task to carry Jesus' message of victory over death and of life everlasting to the other disciples. By carrying out that act, she fulfilled her role and ensured her place in the history of Christianity.

Those are the facts. But there are other stories about Mary Magdalene that may or may not be based on particles of truth. In some cases, these tales are outright fiction. Legends, for example, say that she loved John the Theologian, and his rejection of her caused her to turn to prostitution. In fact, for nearly 2,000 years, she's been portrayed as the Bible's quintessential bad girl—a beautiful, sensuous sinner who heard and heeded Jesus' words, repented, was forgiven, and devoted the rest of her life to Him. It is true she was a sinner. It is also true that she devoted her life to Jesus. But she was never a prostitute, and not a shred of evidence has been found to prove she was.

To understand Mary Magdalene's life, you must first know something about what her world was like, how she came to be maligned, why and how a mythical image of her was formed, and why the myth was perpetuated for centuries. Let's start with the confusion about her name and how she and two other women were lumped into in a composite image of a repentant sinner.

A Much Maligned Mary

Mary has always been a popular choice for a girl's name, even in biblical times. Jesus' mother Mary and Mary, wife of Clopas, both walked with Mary Magdalene on her travels with Jesus. But Jesus had other women followers, and many of them were also named Mary, including Mary Jacobi (mother of James and Joses), Mary Salome, and Mary of Bethany. All these Marys are enough to confuse anyone.

While the New Testament gospel writers singled out these women, mentioning them by name (and thus suggesting their importance in Jesus' life and ministry), other women's names were never revealed. For example, a woman might be referred to as "the woman with the alabaster box" or "the sinner." In fact, the sinner who is mentioned in the quotes that follow is most often confused with Mary Magdalene because of the jar of spikenard (an aromatic ointment) that Mary Magdalene supposedly carried wherever she went.

Now when Jesus was in Bethany, in the house of Simon the leper, there came unto him a woman having an alabaster box of very precious ointment, and poured it on his head as he sat at meat.

—MATTHEW 26:6–7

And behold, a woman in the city, which was a sinner, when she knew that Jesus sat at meat in the Pharisee's house, brought an alabaster box of ointment, and stood at his feet behind him weeping, and began to wash his feet with tears, and did wipe them with the hairs of her head, and kissed his feet, and anointed them with the ointment.

—LUKE 7:37–38

The Gospel of John asserts that this woman who anointed Jesus at the house of Simon the leper was Mary of Bethany.

(It was that Mary which anointed the Lord with ointment, and wiped his feet with her hair, whose brother Lazarus was sick.) —JOHN 11:2

Mary of Bethany was the sister of Martha and Lazarus (whom Jesus raised from the dead). The gospel writers all knew about the anointing at Bethany. Each of them wrote about the same people and incidents that made up Jesus' lifetime and the period immediately following, but sometimes their information conflicted. It can be difficult to sort out individuals and keep all their names straight, especially since Jesus gave new names to many of His disciples and perhaps some of His followers as well.

Nevertheless, the writers of the Bible somehow knew who begat whom and who belonged to which tribe or ethnic lineage. When the gospel writers wrote their stories, they often used an individual's name with that person's place of origin. For example, Mary, Martha, and Lazarus all lived in a house in Bethany, so references to this Mary identify her as Mary of Bethany. In the same way, Jesus was often referred to as Jesus of Nazareth and Mary Magdalene as Mary from Magdala. In the first century,

Although we don't know a great deal about Mary Magdalene's life, here are some interesting details to round out your knowledge of this beloved saint.

Lived: First century

Feast day: July 22

Honorable titles: Thirteenth Apostle, The All, Woman Who Knows the All, and Apostle to the Apostles

Patron saint of: Perfume makers, the contemplative life, repentant sinners, repentant prostitutes, hairdressers, glovers, and the cities of Vézelay, Autun, and Marseilles

Icon: Ointment box or unguent jar

Trivia tidbit: Madeleines are French cookies named after Mary.

Proverb: If it rains on Saint Mary Magdalene's feast day, it will take six weeks to calm her grief.

Veneration: Shrines are dedicated to her at Sainte Maximin-La Sainte-Baume, Provence and at Vezelay, Burgundy.

Magdala, or Migdal Nunya (meaning fish tower), was an unsavory place, equally known for its commercial fishing enterprises and for its prostitution. So Mary of Bethany, Mary of Magdala, and the unnamed sinner became entwined as a composite image of a woman who was a penitent prostitute.

Mary Magdalene's World

There are many gaps in what we know about Mary Magdalene and the circumstances of her life. No mention is made in the Bible of Mary Magdalene's family or whether she was ever married, but we do know that she may have been wealthy. Scholars have said that she was ethnically Jewish, and, as such, she would have been raised to honor and obey Mosaic Laws. And, as mentioned earlier in this chapter, she would have also known her place in the male-dominated Jewish culture in which she lived. Men earned the living, could receive an education, and were allowed to participate fully in the synagogues and courts, whereas women were expected to do the important work of mothering and caring for the home and family.

Jesus never taught His followers to disobey the Torah or to break Jewish law and commandments. Yet, by His example, He taught men how to treat women. To Jesus, women like Mary Magdalene, as well as those who were physically or mentally ill, handicapped, or denigrated and maligned because of their ethnicity, were just as worthy as the ablest and most learned man. Excluding women as priests and church leaders seems to go against the heart of Jesus' message and His example of inclusion. He didn't just tolerate women, He healed them, spoke out when they were unjustly treated, and welcomed them into His inner circle. Mary Magdalene must have embraced His ideas about changing the world through love.

But, as Mary Magdalene would discover after Jesus' death, change—even when it's for the better—doesn't necessarily endure. Take away the leader, and the group may revert to old patterns of behavior. Certainly, there were those in the early Christian community who toyed with the idea of Mary Magdalene and her sisters sharing power and leadership with their brothers in the faith. And as a result, the new Christian community began to splinter, divided over gender equality and the question of whose authority was legitimate—Mary Magdalene's or Peter's—but also over interpretations of Jesus' words, His teachings, and His actions.

The period after Jesus' death was a fractious, inharmonious period in the development of Christianity. The pagan populace around the Mediterranean viewed Christians as rigid and puritanical, while some Jews saw them as mavericks. The Romans tolerated them as just another Jewish sect until A.D. 64, when Nero began widespread persecution targeting Christians. Mary Magdalene, according to one legend, was among those persecuted individuals who fled the Holy Land.

Within the first few centuries, orthodox church leaders must have felt it imperative to unify the divisive factions through the establishment of a creed, canon, and hierarchy. Scholars say these leaders diminished Mary Magdalene's role in the history of the church and did nothing to refute assertions that she was a penitent prostitute. The developing church had to ensure that it could subvert any challenge from within and also from outside forces.

In this crisis of authority, Bishop Ignatius of Antioch in Syria (circa A.D. 107) made it clear for everyone: The bishop was to be revered as though he were God Himself. Further, the hierarchy of power within the church mimicked the hierarchy of Heaven, he told them. He may have taken his cues from a letter written earlier by Clement, Bishop of Rome. In his letter to the Corinthians, Clement reminded Jesus' followers that the apostles got their authority from Jesus Christ, and Jesus got His from God. Clement further noted that just as Jesus had been given His orders and then gave the apostles theirs, so the apostles' followers were supposed to go into the world, preaching as bishops and deacons with the same authority as the apostles (authority granted by God through His son Jesus).

The male Catholic Church hierarchy, thus established, has remained intact until today. Although women of that faith still, after 2,000 years, do not serve in the roles of priests, bishops, or popes, there are those who hope this will change.

The Myth Serves the Church

The image of Mary Magdalene as the harlot who turned away from her old life, sought repentance, and became a devoted follower of Jesus served the newly established church in a couple of ways. First, it was a powerful image for the faith. It carried forth the message that all sinners could enter the kingdom of Heaven if they asked for forgiveness, turned away from sin, were baptized, and accepted Jesus as their Lord. Second, portraying Mary as a former prostitute served to compromise her reputation and any challenge that she and others of her gender might make to the male leadership.

The fact that the early church had problems with unity, leadership, and splinter groups of Christians whose beliefs were deemed heretical fueled this motivation.

During and after Mary's lifetime, the Bible as we know it was being written. Since the selection of texts to be included and excluded wasn't decided until the third century at the Council of Nicaea, Christians before that time learned from those who had been closest to Jesus. Some of Jesus' followers believed in the equality of men and women. They held Mary Magdalene in high regard and may have enjoyed the way she shared Jesus' teachings and thoughtful insights. They may have even been supportive of her role as a leader filling the void that Jesus left.

Such ideology, however, threatened the male church hierarchy that Jesus' more orthodox followers desired. They asserted Peter's right to leadership succession and, by extension, the right of popes as heirs to Peter's role. The modern Roman Catholic Church continues to invoke this rule of papal succession, and it is sometimes used as a rationale for why women cannot be ordained as priests.

In Christianity's early days, there were no church buildings, no collections of sacred texts, no organized system of approved beliefs, and no defined hierarchy of leadership. Men and women simply got together to discuss teachings and to pray. There may have been a consensus that, without a leader, the Jesus movement would not survive, even for a generation. The orthodox among early Christians felt that Jesus, when He was still alive, had picked Simon Peter, His chief male disciple, to be His heir. Yet they could not deny that Mary Magdalene, a loving companion and confidante, had enjoyed the closest relationship with Jesus.

Still, it's not hard to understand why the male disciples must have also believed that Jesus would never have permitted a woman to be the head of His church. Women were treated as inferiors in biblical times, and they weren't afforded any of the same freedoms and privileges as men. How on earth, the disciples must have wondered, could a *woman* carry Jesus' legacy into the world and to subsequent generations?

Mary Magdalene's relationship with Peter was clearly challenging. Maybe that tension had more to do with Peter's dislike of women in general than any specific antagonism he had toward Mary Magdalene. However, the Pistis Sophia, a text excluded from the Bible, has revealed that Peter did have his complaints about Mary. For one thing, he didn't like all of Mary's questions to Jesus. He thought she talked too much and that all of her talking took time away from the men in the group.

In Mary Magdalene's lifetime, women learned early that in some situations they were expected to hold their tongues, be discreet, and choose their words carefully. Women were never supposed to upstage men or usurp their power in synagogues and in places where communal prayers were said. It is unlikely that anyone other than Jesus ever would have offered Mary Magdalene an important leadership position in the early church. As a woman out preaching, she must have been fully aware of the consequences of her actions: persecution and even, possibly, death. Nevertheless, she continued to share the faith and preach Jesus' message of love and redemption.

How the Myth Was Made

In A.D. 591, Pope Gregory I was working on a homily, and he needed a model to represent Christianity's forgiving and transformative nature. He recalled the image of the promiscuous woman who, because she had "loved much" (a phrase often interpreted literally), had wiped Jesus' feet with her unbound hair in violation of Jewish rabbinical norms of behavior. In homily number thirty-three, Pope Gregory I merged the repentant Mary Magdalene with the woman who had the alabaster jar. The Gospel of Luke dubbed her the sinful woman, while only the Gospel of John referred to her as Mary of Bethany. In linking these two portraits, Pope Gregory I ensured that the composite image would stick to Mary Magdalene for a long time.

> *She whom Luke calls the sinful woman, whom John calls Mary, we believe to be the Mary from whom seven devils were ejected according to Mark. And what did these seven devils signify, if not all the vices? . . . It is clear, brothers, that the woman previously used the unguent to perfume her flesh acts.*
>
> —GREGORY I: HOMILY XXXIII

What was Pope Gregory thinking? Was he being clever, careless, or just shortsighted? Was he emphasizing what others already believed? Did he view women as highly impressionable, perhaps foolish, and morally and spiritually inferior to men? We can only speculate. Various scholars have asserted that the making of the myth was intentional and that it served the pope's purpose. It illustrated his point in showing how forgiving Christianity can be toward those who commit the vilest of sins.

The Gnostics' Portrayal of Mary Magdalene

Previously in this chapter, you learned that the early Christian Church became somewhat fragmented in the years following Jesus' death and resurrection. The Gnostics were one such fragment. These believers also wrote accounts of Jesus' life and ministry, but their writings were excluded from the Bible because their beliefs diverged from orthodox ideas. It seems the Gnostics had a different role in mind for Mary Magdalene.

The word Gnostic derives from the word *gnosis*, meaning "mystical knowledge." Some of the Gnostic literature may predate the New Testament Gospels, and in these texts Mary Magdalene is exalted. The Gnostics saw her as the Embodiment of Wisdom and the Sacred Feminine. Their texts, which include the Gospel of Mary, the Pistis Sophia, the Gospel of Thomas, and others, contain ideas the early church fathers didn't support. These writings also flesh out the image of Mary Magdalene, although not fully.

BELIEFS OF THE FIRST CENTURY GNOSTICS

The early Gnostics had a unique set of beliefs that included the following:

- Salvation comes from inner work rather than from outside forces.
- Light or divine soul is trapped in matter or darkness.
- Inner divine knowledge (*gnosis*) liberates the soul.
- Jesus is the divine messenger bearing *gnosis* to humans.
- The soul of each human is divine; the body is polluted.
- The powers of spiritual awakening include visions, dreams, and inspired speaking and writing.

- God has a feminine side.
- Men and women are equal (women held liturgical, leadership positions).
- Sophia (divine wisdom) is the spirit part of God.
- The dead are resurrected.
- Living a righteous life leads to salvation.
- When trapped in matter (the physical world), the soul suffers.

The Pistis Sophia shows Mary Magdalene as Jesus' insightful chief questioner. She shines as someone who is spiritually adept and who embodies wisdom. In the Gospel of Thomas also, Mary Magdalene is shown to be inquisitive. Although Peter tells those gathered that Mary Magdalene should leave because she is female, Jesus tells Peter that He will guide her to become a spirit more like a male's so she will be fit to enter Heaven. Lest any females take offense at this, it's important to note that scholars assert "male" stands as a metaphor for divine. Jesus will make Mary Magdalene less female (human) to become more male (divine).

NAG HAMMADI TREASURES

Copies of the Gnostic gospels, including the Gospel of Mary, Pistis Sophia, and Apocryphon of John, were among the fifty-two texts discovered in 1945 in a clay jar found near Nag Hammadi, Egypt. Peasants found the jar in one of the more than 150 caves in the Jabal al-Tārif mountain. The texts shed new light on the beginning of Christianity in first-century Palestine. In particular, scholars have used the version of the Gospel of Mary found at Nag Hammadi to supplement two other copies known to exist. In 1896, Dr. Carl Reinhardt, a German scholar, purchased a copy of the Gospel of Mary from a manuscript peddler in Cairo and took it to Berlin to study. Dr. Reinhardt's translation was not published until 1955.

You can find a comprehensive list of the manuscripts found at Nag Hammadi, including the Gospel of Mary (no complete version of this gospel exists) and other Gnostic works, on the Internet at *www.gnosis.org* and in the book *The Nag Hammadi Library, The Definitive Translation of the Gnostic Scriptures Complete in One Volume*, edited by James M. Robinson.

In the Dialogue of the Savior, yet another Gnostic text, Jesus calls Mary Magdalene the Woman Who Knows the All. In the Gospel of Philip, Mary Magdalene and Jesus are portrayed as being so close that Jesus often kisses her on the lips, much to the consternation of Peter and the other disciples. Finally, in the Gospel of Mary, she is shown to be a spiritual conduit for Jesus' words. After the Lord has left the earth, Mary Magdalene, who must have been deeply grieving herself, comforts the disciples who have hidden, fearing for their lives. She also shares a special teaching that the Lord gave her in a vision, turning the disciples' thoughts away from negativity and back to goodness and optimism. She becomes the "glue" that holds the fledgling church together.

Legends and Scholarly Speculation

The name Mary, spoken in the Aramaic language of Jesus, becomes Miryam. Mary Magdalene was variously called Miryam of Magdala and Mary of Migdal, as well as Mary Magdalene. The New Testament Gospels reveal nothing about Mary Magdalene's youth, but popular stories suggest she was beautiful and came from a wealthy family. The Bible says she and other women provided for Jesus and His followers out of their personal resources. Since husbands, children, and other family members are not mentioned, scholars suggest that Mary Magdalene may have banded with other Jewish women who set out on their own to follow Jesus. Whenever Jesus walked along the hot, rock-strewn dusty roads between the villages in Judea and Galilee, Mary Magdalene would likely have been alongside Him.

Mary Magdalene's seven demons, as the Bible describes them, might have been epilepsy or a form of mental illness. Some say her demons were vices accrued from her prior sensual life and lack of morality. The seven devils, or demons, could also symbolize the age-old vices of gluttony, lust, sloth, pride, anger, envy, and covetousness. Biblical writers of both the Old Testament and New Testament frequently used the number seven, considered sacred, to suggest exaggeration, something extreme, or completion. Thus the devils, numbering seven, might have been so exaggerated or complete that Mary Magdalene was fully "possessed" by them. If her possession was epilepsy, it is likely that it was an extreme form. Seven also represents wisdom, contemplation, and a sacred inner life of "knowing." Perhaps she had visions or heard voices that she (and others) did not fully comprehend, which contributed to her being labeled as possessed.

Theories abound as to what happened to her after Jesus died. She may have fled the Holy Land to escape persecution. Neither the apostle Paul's writings nor the Acts of the Apostles, which details the church's development from Jesus' resurrection to Paul's imprisonment, mentions Mary Magdalene. One popular orthodox legend suggests that Mary Magdalene accompanied St. John the Evangelist (also referred to as the Beloved Disciple) to Ephesus, where the two preached to the locals. Another legend says her persecutors put her and other Christians in a boat without oars and set it adrift on the Mediterranean Sea. These Christians arrived on the shore of southern France, where Mary Magdalene preached for a while and was so loved that churches were erected in her honor. Eventually, she became a contemplative living in a cave known as La Sainte-Baume, where she pondered divine mysteries. One well-known story says that she survived until she was seventy-two, eating only one Holy Eucharist wafer each day, served to her by angels.

Mary Magdalene may have felt a deep and immediate spiritual connection to Jesus. To walk away from whatever life she had in order to follow Jesus must have required her to release any fear of the unknown and be open to change. Her decision speaks volumes about her strong spirit, determination, and commitment to Him. She did not let others' gossip and criticisms keep her from following Him. When she decided to let go of her old life to embrace the new one, she must have known things would never be the same.

Now, under the microscope of Christian feminists, religious historians, and biblical scholars, Mary Magdalene's life is being conscientiously reviewed and cautiously revised. Her name has been cleared as well. In 1969, the Vatican reversed its position on Mary Magdalene being a prostitute. It officially separated the combined Mary Magdalene and Mary of Bethany stories and revised its missal. More recently, Pope John Paul II acknowledged Mary Magdalene, bestowing upon her the title of Apostle to the Apostles, one of her most sacred and important roles.

Ways to Invoke the Holy Blessings of Saint Mary Magdalene

Throughout this book, you'll find invocations to venerate Saint Mary Magdalene and bring her blessings of goodness and grace into your life. For each chapter, you can do as many of these as you choose.

Buy some frankincense and myrrh or rose-scented anointing oil. Use it to anoint yourself, your family, and your friends, since it is considered a blessing to both those being anointed and the one doing the anointing. You can "anoint," which means smear or rub, by making the sign of the cross on the forehead. This is an effective way to invite Saint Mary Magdalene to join you in a period of devotional prayer, meditation, and contemplation. If your devotional period involves saying the rosary, anoint the top of the hand in which you hold the prayer beads. Let the scent calm you and call you to holiness, drawing you deeply inward to a contemplative state. In the beginning, it may be useful to visualize the image of Saint Mary Magdalene with an unguent jar as she might have anointed Jesus.

Read *The Gnostic Gospels* by Elaine Pagels. Find out about the books that were excluded from the Bible and why. Discover what was written in the Gnostic texts. Meditate, pray, and discuss what you learn with others in order to open your mind and heart to the world of Saint Mary Magdalene.

Affirmations

- ✷ I seek to dwell in the company of Saint Mary Magdalene, blessed among women, beloved of Jesus, exemplar to women of all times and places.

- ✷ Each day, I will set aside time to ponder the ways you, Saint Mary Magdalene, served our Lord Jesus and how I might emulate your good works and love for Him.

Form a discussion group. Share knowledge with others about Saint Mary Magdalene's life and her interactions with Jesus. Create a context and framework for your questions by reading about the political climate swirling around the world of Judaism during Jesus' lifetime. Consider the challenges facing Saint Mary Magdalene and the early Christians after His death. Ask each person to bring a question about the life of Mary. Use those questions as departure points for future discussions.

Make a diptych altarpiece. Cut two panels out of a thick piece of foam board and use tape to hinge the pieces together. Or, instead, purchase (or make) two small wooden panels and affix metal hinges to hold them together. On the front of each panel, paste holy cards or beautiful images of Jesus and Saint Mary Magdalene. Further decorate the work using a pen with gold ink to create an iconographic pattern around the images (you can find decorative pattern books in the craft section of bookstores). You can decoupage the images that are on the wood panels, if you like. Think of the Lord and Saint Mary Magdalene as you make this item for your altar. It has been said that when you do an activity with devotion, the Lord is present, and He makes your hands holy to do His work. Have your priest bless the altarpiece.

Affirmations

✿ *I will open my ears, heart, and mind the way Saint Mary Magdalene did to learn the lessons the Lord teaches me through others.*

BLESSED SAINT MARY MAGDALENE, whose beauty and light were pleasing to our Lord and whom He healed and made whole, we honor you. Oh blessed saint, you, who hurried to His tomb to anoint His broken body with your perfumed unguents on Easter morning, inspire us to love the Lord the way you did with intensity, loyalty, and fearless commitment. Glorious Saint Mary Magdalene, we ask you to pray for us and with us to Lord Jesus Christ that He give us the sight to see and the strength to know how to cast out our demons. Let us never be lost but always keep our eyes fixed steadfastly on the ways of the Lord. Let our minds be ever thoughtful of the teachings of the Lord. And let our hearts be overflowing with the sacred love that you shared with Jesus. Thank you, blessed Saint Mary Magdalene, for hearing our petitions and interceding on our behalf to our Lord. Amen.

CHAPTER 2

SECRETS, SPECULATION, AND SACRED SEXUALITY

They said to him, "Why do you love her more than all of us?" The savior answered and said to them, "Why do I not love you like her? When a blind man and one who sees are both together in the darkness, they are no different from one another. When the light comes, then he who sees will see the light, and he who is blind will remain in darkness."
—GOSPEL OF PHILIP, *THE NAG HAMMADI LIBRARY*

Does the Bible contain a secret about Mary and Jesus? Are we to believe that Mary and Jesus loved each other, shared a special bond that went beyond friendship, and might have been married, as suggested in *The Da Vinci Code* and other popular books? Undoubtedly, the fully human Mary Magdalene longed for love. It would take nothing away from Jesus' divinity if, in fact, the speculation were to prove true. It would in no way diminish the Church's historical position. Wanting to love and be loved is a natural urge. The Church has always acknowledged Jesus' humanity and divinity as equally important, and in scripture we see Jesus display a full range of human emotions.

What is it about falling in love that makes us feel so euphoric, so special, so committed that we can pledge our affection and allegiance to another individual forever? Some say love is a sacred energy that moves easily between souls who share an attraction for one another. Others say that God is love and that His love is expressed through us in myriad ways, including romantic, altruistic, and parental affection. Allowing ourselves to be conduits for love magnifies us and, as physicians tell us, increases our energy and life force. Closing our hearts to others because of a self-centered focus chokes love and diminishes our own well-being.

We know how love often begins—a glance, a touch, a kind word. So how did the love between Mary and Jesus—romantic or otherwise—first begin to grow? Mary Magdalene possibly met Jesus in a village near the Sea of Galilee, where He often traveled. He may have caught her attention when He did not cross to the other side of the road as she approached, when He gazed upon her with compassionate eyes, or when He did not turn away because of her illness, which others may have thought made her unclean or imperfect. Perhaps she had already heard of this preacher, the Nazarene. Maybe He had already heard of her, one of the wealthy women in Magdala.

Or perhaps they were total strangers until that day when their paths crossed, and taking note of her affliction, He healed her. Mary was surely grateful. It is possible that a deep current of unconditional love flowed from Him and catalyzed her feelings. That spark of holy love kindled in her a divine flame. Mary Magdalene thereafter placed her body and soul in service to Jesus. She treasured His gift of love and praised the giver.

The quote from the Gospel of Philip, which opens this chapter, suggests the disciples are concerned about the nature of Jesus' affection toward Mary Magdalene and the fact that He kissed her often. This led them to ask if He loved her more than them. They weren't blind to the display of affection, but they did not fully comprehend the special bond between the Lord and Mary Magdalene. They may also have felt jealous.

Michael Baigent, Richard Leigh, and Henry Lincoln's book *Holy Blood, Holy Grail* and the novel and movie of Dan Brown's *The Da Vinci Code* weave together disparate threads of oral storytelling, facts, inference, myth, legend, and outright speculation about the relationship between Mary Magdalene and Jesus. For some readers, the books are shockingly controversial, especially for those readers who have no previous exposure to such stories as Jesus having a twin brother or escaping the Crucifixion while someone named Simon of Cyrene took His place. Other possibilities may seem even more strange, like the stories that Mary Magdalene and Jesus were involved in a romantic relationship and that the Holy Grail was *not* the cup Jesus drank from at the Last Supper but instead was that of Mary Magdalene, who was married to Jesus. Equally provocative is the assertion that their child Sarah established the royal blood line of the Merovingian dynasty in France and that secret societies of the Church concealed such "heresies" while some of the members died protecting and passing on "proof" to subsequent generations.

Such tales may have some basis in truth, but the facts to support these suppositions are, at best, unclear. The canonical gospels (those sanctioned for inclusion in the Bible) mention neither kisses between Mary and Jesus nor a marriage between them that produced children. The writers' silence on the subject of Jesus' love for Mary Magdalene leads to speculation but offers no facts.

If Mary Magdalene and Jesus had shared a romance, would their lives have been any less sacred? On the other hand, if evidence were ever found to support the speculation that they were married, it would effectively challenge the Church's position on sex and marriage for holy men (priests). And the significance of Mary Magdalene's roles as wife and church leader would beg the question of modern women's roles in positions of church authority. Yet without concrete evidence of a romantic involvement, scholars and others can only speculate.

Ambiguity and Supposition

The Bible is full of ambiguity. Mary Magdalene often listened to Jesus speaking in parables rich in symbolism and pregnant with meaning. From our Sunday school lessons, we have heard the approved New Testament versions of Jesus' teachings and sayings. If we read them for ourselves, the lessons, depending on the Bible we use and the translation, may seem simplistic and straightforward. We assume this is what Jesus intended—to make His teachings accessible to anyone with ears to listen.

Yet, when we read the Gnostic Gospels, we learn that even the inner circle of disciples sometimes could not fathom the subtle meaning of certain teachings. Mary Magdalene was different. Not only was she able to offer insights into meaning, she also capably served as a spokeswoman articulating Jesus' words. Always, she gave credit to the Lord for everything good and holy that flowed through her, including her understanding of truth. In the Gospel of Mary, she related a secret esoteric teaching about the rise of the soul that Jesus had given her in a vision. Challenged by Andrew and hotly contested by Peter, Mary was reduced to tears. While Peter and Andrew may have viewed Mary Magdalene as a "typical emotional woman," Jesus saw her as the perfect disciple, a fitting receptacle to hold His words. She was a conduit for His sacred teachings and a powerful witness for the faith. Jesus knew that Mary Magdalene would love Him for all eternity. When He, the Light of the World, was no longer in human form, Mary Magdalene would become a holy prism reflecting His light.

As long as I [Jesus] am in the world, I am the light of the world.

—JOHN 9:5

The New Testament Gospels focus on Mary Magdalene as a fallen woman redeemed. From reading Chapter 1, we understand how and why Pope Gregory I (also known as Pope Gregory the Great) mythologized her in this way. In contrast, other gospels and Gnostic texts written around the same time or before the New Testament Gospels depict Mary Magdalene, not as a rich harlot, but as a thoughtful, intimate companion of Jesus. Gnostics, in their gospels as well as in their practice, accorded women an elevated stature. Feminine imagery and symbols permeate Gnostic writing, so it is understandable that Mary Magdalene, for them, could have been viewed as a potent female counterpoint to Jesus, the Son of Man, as they sometimes called Him. The Gnostics accepted the belief that in deep contemplation and meditation, spiritual aspirants might receive teachings through visions and intuitive knowledge. Mary certainly had visions and had leanings toward the contemplative life. We know this much from stories and legends about her.

MISSING WORDS CONTRIBUTE TO CONFUSION

In the Gospel of Philip, the piece of papyri with the sentence telling readers where Jesus kissed Mary Magdalene is unfortunately missing. Although He might have kissed her on the lips and, in fact, most scholars complete the sentence with the word "lips," the kiss could also have been on her hair, her eyes, or any other part of her body. Wherever Jesus kissed Mary Magdalene, however, it made Peter and the other disciples jealous.

Words are missing in many places in the Gospel of Philip and also in the Gospel of Mary. Translators and scholars have filled in missing words by placing what they believe to be the most appropriate words in brackets. There are three copies, all fragments, of the Gospel of Mary in existence. No complete copy of the entire gospel, written sometime in the second century, is known to have survived. A damaged fragment of the Gospel of Mary having only twenty lines and called Papyrus Oxyrhynchus 3525 was excavated in a town by the same name in Egypt. It dates to the early third century A.D., and the writing is in a Greek cursive script. Another piece of the Gospel of Mary turned up in papyri fragments in 1896 when Dr. Carol Reinhardt, a German scholar, purchased the manuscript from a peddler in Cairo. The third piece is called the Papyrus Rylands 463, and it surfaced in 1917. Even after putting all the versions together, the Gospel of Mary is less than eight pages long and constitutes about half of what scholars believe to be the length of the original book. Even so, the work contributes enough new information to have given rise to a flurry of books by scholars offering commentary on Mary Magdalene's roles as apostolic leader and as a source of inspiration for men and women in the Jesus movement.

Questions about Marriage

Many modern books that postulate a romantic involvement between Mary Magdalene and Jesus rely on the Gnostic gospels, Grail legends, and what the Bible does *not* say. For example, nowhere in the New Testament Gospels does it say Jesus was a single man. Also, the virtual lack of detail about Mary Magdalene, when it is obvious from what we *are* told that she was someone of importance, leads to many unanswered questions. Chief among them is, why did the gospel writers not say that Jesus and Mary were married or simply state that they were *not* married? This important fact was excluded from all four of the New Testament Gospels, but characters of lesser importance were listed as wives of certain male followers. The kiss in the Gospel of Philip suggests a subtext to the Mary and Jesus story, but there is still no definitive answer in the Gnostic writings.

Mary Magdalene may have herself embraced Gnostic ideas. Though not all Gnostics were in agreement about affirming women, there were those who believed that the female was not inferior to the male. Orthodox believers, alternatively, tended to accept the superiority of man and the subjugation of woman based on the book of Genesis, which says that Eve was made after Adam and from his rib, although some have asserted the imperfection was in Adam's body.

The Gnostic mind, on the other hand, could elevate a woman to the level of divinity; after all, many believed that God was both feminine and masculine. In the mind of the Gnostics, was Mary Magdalene the embodiment of the Divine Feminine, consort of the Christ, as some feminist scholars assert? These early Christians in their writings depicted Mary Magdalene as a spiritually mature woman, full of wisdom, compassion, love, and tenderness. She could be withdrawn, prayerful, and contemplative. You can just imagine her huddled close to Jesus, speaking thoughtfully and perhaps smiling, her dark eyes reflecting the light of her holiness.

The idea of a love union between Mary and Jesus reflects a universal longing for balance between masculine and feminine, according to feminist scholars. There were many Romans and others during Mary Magdalene's time who did not believe in the one God of the Jews and Christians. These people worshipped pagan gods who had consorts or goddesses. The logical goddess or consort of Jesus, some believe, was Mary Magdalene. She was clearly His favorite female disciple.

Some of the apostles, including Simon Peter, for example, had wives. Paul, in his first letter to the Christians in Corinth, makes a case for marriage, noting that several of the apostles were married. If he had himself wished to marry, he might have brought up the Lord's name as an example of someone who was. But Paul never uses that argument.

Martin Luther, the German theologian and leader of the Protestant Reformation, may have believed that Mary Magdalene was married to Jesus, since in his First Psalm Lectures in 1515, he made mention of Mary Magdalene calling out "for her husband much more wonderfully in spirit than in body." Brigham Young, second prophet of the Church of Jesus Christ of Latter Day Saints (known as the Mormon church), may have also believed Mary Magdalene was Jesus' wife. According to Kay Nichols, a practicing Mormon whose husband Bud is an elder, "Mormons believe that you need to have a mate in order to create eternal families in God's kingdom. Those who die before they have a companion will have a mate in Heaven. And the most logical person to have been Jesus' mate was Mary Magdalene," she said, adding, "It's a commonly held belief among Mormons but is not a doctrine of the church."

So we are led to speculate. We do know that Mary Magdalene was Jesus' closest companion. Perhaps that was enough. Her proximity to Jesus also leads us to ponder her connection to the Holy Grail.

Mary Magdalene and the Holy Grail

What exactly is the Holy Grail, and where is it today? Some Grail legends suggest it was the chalice that captured the blood of Christ as it fell from His body on the cross. Others say it was the cup Jesus drank from at the Last Supper and passed around to each of His disciples. According to the tale, mentioned earlier, that Mary Magdalene's persecutors placed her in a boat without oars and set the boat adrift on the sea, she may have had the Grail with her when she crossed the Mediterranean to the French coastal village of Les Saintes Maries de la Mer.

The heretical explanation, however, and the one revealed in *The Da Vinci Code* is that she—Mary Magdalene—*was* the Holy Grail, the vessel that carried the *Sangreal* (Holy Grail in Medieval French) or *sangraal* (from the Latin *sanguin* or blood). The French word for blood is *sang*, so one might say she was carrying the royal blood or holy blood of Jesus, as inferred in the books *Holy Blood, Holy Grail* and *The Da Vinci Code*. The latter work characterizes the idea of a married Mary Magdalene and Jesus as the great secret that could have undermined the papacy. The Knights Templar, a religious and militaristic order created by the Priory of Sion (a secret society supposedly founded by the French king Godefroi de Bouillon in 1099) became responsible for protecting the secret along with the couple's marriage documentation, hidden under the Temple of Jerusalem.

However, writers Hank Hanegraaff and Paul L. Maier, authors of *The Da Vinci Code, Fact or Fiction,* dispute novelist Dan Brown's assertion that Jesus and Mary were ever married and that the Priory of Sion is anything but a modern organization. The authors reveal in their book that documents in Paris's Bibliotheque Nationale that supposedly prove the existence of the Priory of Sion are part of a hoax perpetrated by a colorful character named Pierre Plantard. They assert that, with the help of an associate, Plantard (who had been convicted of fraud) fabricated the genealogical lists and documents naming Priory grand masters. According to the authors, the true Priory of Sion was a social group founded in 1956.

Furthermore, they dispute that the burning of some of the Templars at the stake, including Grand Master Jacques de Molay in 1314, was at the pope's behest, as suggested in *The Da Vinci Code.* Rather, it was the doing of the France's King Philip. They say that the king pressured the pope to suppress the order simply out of greed—the king wanted the Templars' wealth.

In *Holy Blood, Holy Grail,* which serves as one of the sources for Dan Brown's novel, the scenario depicts a married Mary Magdalene with at least one child in tow secretly entering France and seeking refuge in a Jewish community. According to this theory, Jesus and Mary's child, named Sarah, is the ancestress of the bloodline for some Merovingian royals. (The Merovingians were a Frankish dynasty that ruled circa A.D. 450–751.) For the next 400 years, Mary Magdalene and Jesus' bloodline continued as their descendants intermarried with Romans, Jews, Visigoths, and so forth. Having put forth the idea, the authors then deem the whole scenario preposterous, claiming it is based on too few facts and a flimsy foundation.

The legend of the Holy Grail surfaced at the end of the twelfth century—one of the darkest periods of civilization. It was also a time in the Church's history when Mary Magdalene's popularity swelled to great heights. The story of the Grail, or mythological sacred chalice, was a product of the creative genius of a man named Chrêtien de Troyes. Like a bestseller of the time, his story spread across Europe with the rapidity of an airborne virus. The Grail soon became an important symbol of Christianity. Its popularity was highest during the period of the Crusades, ranging from A.D. 1095 to 1148. That powerful symbol heralded the beginning of a spiritual revival across the European continent.

During this time, Mary Magdalene's cult likely flourished in the Languedoc-Roussillon region of France, particularly in the city of Beziers, which had its own Mary Magdalene church. The area became known as a magnet for heretics, especially the Cathars, a Christian sect in Western Europe during the twelfth and thirteenth centuries. Like many of the Gnostics, Cathars believed in equality between males and females. They felt it was their duty to purify themselves and to live clean lives. They embraced ideas of the Divine Feminine. Their simplicity of faith and lifestyle attracted many followers, and this popularity was a threat to the Church, which at that time was suffering from accusations of excesses.

The Cathars and Their Beliefs

The Cathars used the ancient stone citadel on top of a mountain at Montségur as a meditation site (and, some say, a protective haven to house the sacred Grail). Later, they reconfigured and fortified the citadel for protection against assaults by Crusaders, to whom it fell in 1244. Following are some other interesting facts about this medieval sect.

- They were Gnostics and called the Pure Ones because their name derives from the Greek word *katharos* meaning "pure."

- The Cathars were vegetarians and pacifists who advocated resisting all forms of tyranny, whether religious or secular.

- They believed that humans have a body, soul, and spirit. The soul lives in the body and the spirit (which is a spark of the divine) dwells in the soul.

- They felt spiritual purity was of paramount importance if their spirit's divine spark was to return to its source, the Light (God).

- They established prosperous communities that focused on the spirit of cooperation and self-sufficiency, and they abhorred the Church's excess.

- Their most spiritually advanced masters were known as Perfects or Parfaits (and included women).

- They worshipped on mountaintops or in forests.

- They shunned the material world and the veneration of material objects, including the relics of saints and the icon of the cross.

- They believed in reincarnation.

- To them, Jesus was cosmic and therefore could not have died on the cross.

- They felt the Roman Catholic Church had altered many of the early Christian teachings for its own gain.

- They believed the spirit grew stronger through prayer and spiritual purity.

At the heart of the problem for the Cathars, however, was their refusal to acknowledge the pope's supreme authority. Authors Lynn Picknett and Clive Prince in their book *The Templar Revelation* explain that after trying many different tactics to root out the Cathars and the ordinary Catholics who were their sympathizers and supporters, Pope Innocent III ordered a crusade—the first to pit Christians against Christians. On Mary Magdalene's feast day, July 22, thousands of Cathars and the townspeople who supported them died in a massacre that marked the beginning of the Abigensian Crusade.

Crusaders, including knights and the bishops in charge, might have stopped the assault against the Cathars at Beziers in 1209, but they didn't. The man reporting back to Pope Innocent III declared that they had killed them all and that God would recognize those who were heretics and those who weren't. The Crusade continued until 1244, culminating with the siege of a stone citadel atop a mountain in Montségur. Thus the forces that quashed the Gnostics centuries earlier purged the Cathars as well. The Inquisition soon followed. If ever the world needed someone who could embody light, beauty, grace, and leadership—someone such as Mary Magdalene—it was during the twelfth and thirteenth centuries. The world was in dire need of healing.

The Marriage at Cana

Proponents of the theory that Mary Magdalene and Jesus were married point to a Jewish convention in existence during the couple's lifetime. A Jewish man was expected to marry and create children. By not marrying,

Jesus would have willingly chosen to go against societal norms and practices under Mosaic Law.

Some say precedent existed for Him to choose bachelorhood. For example, some prophets of the Old Testament and His own cousin, John the Baptist, did not marry. Yet, those who believe that He would have married suggest that by not marrying, the society in which He lived would have judged Him to be diminished. His own grandfather Saint Joachim, suffered terribly for being barren until God's mercy enabled Joachim's wife Anne to become pregnant with Mary, the Blessed Virgin. The temple priests of Joachim's time refused his offering, calling him cursed by God for not fathering children (in particular, sons).

As for being a wife, Mary Magdalene may not have wanted marriage either. It is likely, however, that she would have been deeply attracted to the charismatic Jesus. How could she not have fallen in love with Him? But would Jesus have returned her love as a man to a woman? Or would He have subjugated His more human instincts in order to devote all of His body's energy and power to His divine mission? Or was Mary Magdalene a teacher for Him, initiating Him in sacred rites of lovemaking, perhaps toward the goal of merging male and female energies into a mystical state of cosmic consciousness where their sense of separateness dissolved into an ocean of oneness?

And he answered and said unto them, Have ye not read, that he which made them at the beginning made them male and female; and said, For this cause shall a man leave father and mother, and shall cleave to his wife: and they twain shall be one flesh?

—MATTHEW 19:4–5

God knew exactly what He was doing when He created male and female. Further, He may have had a specific purpose in mind—marriage. Mary Magdalene cherished Jesus. Some writers have suggested that the wedding at Cana was none other than Mary Magdalene's own wedding to Jesus. He was there with His disciples. Mary Magdalene might have been there as well since she traveled with Him and His followers, although others point out that this does not fit the Gospels' timeline. At many weddings today, it is the mother of the bride or groom who most often worries about the quantities of food and drink. In this story, Jesus' own mother seems to be the one doing this sort of worrying. She's a guest at this wedding (or so we are to believe), and yet she goes to the servants of the house and tells them to carry out Jesus' instructions. In her instruction to the servants, she effectively orchestrates what will be Jesus' first sign that He is the Messiah.

And when they wanted wine, the mother of Jesus saith unto him, They have no wine.

Jesus saith unto her, Woman, what have I to do with thee? Mine hour is not yet come.

His mother saith unto the servants, Whatsoever he saith unto you, do it.

And there were set there six waterpots of stone, after the manner of the purifying of the Jews, containing two or three firkins apiece.

Jesus saith unto them, Fill the waterpots with water. And they filled them up to the brim.

And he saith unto them, Draw out now, and bear unto the governor of the feast. And they bare it.

When the ruler of the feast had tasted the water that was made wine, and knew not whence it was, (but the servants which drew the water knew,) the governor of the feast called the bridegroom,

And saith unto him, Every man at the beginning doth set forth good wine; and when men have well drunk, then that which is worse: but thou has kept the good wine until now.

—JOHN 2:3–10

Mary Magdalene and The Last Supper

When taken to another level, the idea of Mary Magdalene being partners with Jesus (either as a wife or divine consort) suggests that she stands as the embodiment of the Sacred Feminine and He, the Sacred Masculine. The famous Italian painter Leonardo Da Vinci may have known about the symbology of the feminine. Indeed, Da Vinci was a visionary, a man ahead of his time, who conveyed many controversial ideas through his art.

Best-selling author Dan Brown (*The Da Vinci Code, Angels and Demons*, and others) said in media interviews following publication of his book *The Da Vinci Code* that he believes that Mary Magdalene is present in Leonardo Da Vinci's portrait of *The Last Supper*. In *The Da Vinci Code*, Brown instructs readers to examine *The Last Supper* and look for the "V" created by the positions of disciples' bodies to the right of Jesus. The letter "V" stands for the Sacred Feminine. The symbol of *hieros gamos*, sacred marriage, is a six-pointed star. One-half of the star is made by a "V." The other half of the star is a pyramid, a male symbol of power.

Interconnect the "V" with the pyramid, and they form the Star of David (Jesus was a descendant of the House of David—Matthew 1:1), the seal of Solomon, and, of course, the symbol of *hieros gamos*. Da Vinci's *The Last Supper* could reflect the artist's beliefs regarding the importance of Mary in Jesus' inner circle—that she was the wife of Jesus and was also the Holy Grail, a human chalice to contain the Savior's bloodline.

MARY MAGDALENE'S FOLLOWING IN FRANCE

Holy Grail, Mystical Bride, Divine Feminine—regardless of her titles and how she is venerated, Mary Magdalene has a following even today along France's southern shore, where numerous statues, grottos, churches, and shrines dedicated to her stand as witness to a woman of great spiritual stature in her own right.

In Da Vinci's tableau depicting the Last Supper, the person known as the Beloved Disciple (thought by many to be the youngest, John) appears outwardly effeminate. Could this figure instead be Mary Magdalene? A smaller, close-up sketch of this figure shows it to be distinctly that of a woman with a beautiful face, long, thick hair, loving eyes, and a sweet mouth. Da Vinci was painting the last supper the disciples shared with Jesus, and it is likely that Mary was there. Perhaps, as a good Jewish woman or wife would do, she covered her hair, lit the Sabbath candles, and made sure that unleavened bread and wine were on the table. Possibly, she even served and partook of that last meal with her beloved Jesus.

Speculation about the Beloved Disciple

The unnamed disciple whom Jesus loved makes appearances in the New Testament Gospels but, for some reason, is never named. In the Gospel of John, the gospel writer says that the one whom Jesus loved leaned on His chest during the last meal the disciples shared with their Lord.

Now there was leaning on Jesus' bosom one of his disciples, whom Jesus loved.

—JOHN 13:23

The Gospel of John's narrator reveals that Jesus had a mysterious role for this one whom He loved, and He would not reveal it to Peter. Peter asked Jesus to explain.

Peter seeing him saith to Jesus, Lord, and what shall this man do?

Jesus saith unto him, If I will that he tarry till I come, what is that to thee? Follow thou me.

Then went this saying abroad among the brethren, that that disciple should not die: yet Jesus said not unto him, He shall not die; but, If I will that he tarry till I come, what is that to thee?

—JOHN 21:21–23

Differences of opinion abound regarding the identity of this unnamed disciple. The Gospel of John asserts that this one "whom Jesus loved" stayed with Jesus' mother at the foot of the cross (we know Mary Magdalene was there with Jesus' mother Mary), even while the other disciples fled and hid. Further, when told that Jesus' body was gone from the grave, the beloved disciple and Peter raced to the tomb, but the disciple got there first and then had the distinction of being the first to believe. The Gospels of Matthew and Mark reveal that Mary was the first to see the risen Christ. Luke says it was a group of women that included Mary Magdalene. John says it was Mary alone. Perhaps because of this, people make a connection between Mary Magdalene, the one we know Jesus loved more than the others, and this unnamed disciple. So we have wild speculation, but no conclusive proof, that Mary Magdalene was the disciple whom Jesus loved. The writer of the Gospel of John says, however, that Mary carried the message of the empty tomb to Peter *and* to the one whom Jesus loved, which seems to make it pretty clear, at least in the Gospel of John, that Mary was delivering the message to this unnamed person, who many speculate was John.

The first day of the week cometh Mary Magdalene early, when it was yet dark, unto the sepulchre; and seeth the stone taken away from the sepulchre.

Then she runneth, and cometh to Simon Peter, and to the other disciple, whom Jesus loved, and saith unto them, They have taken away the Lord out of the sepulchre, and we know not where they have laid him.

Peter therefore went forth, and that other disciple, and came to the sepulchre.

So they ran both together: and the other disciple did outrun Peter, and came first to the sepulchre.

—JOHN 20:1:4

Because in biblical times women did not have power, the opportunity to earn a wage, a social stature on a par with men, or, in many cases, the ability to read and write, it might make sense to think that Jesus would have chosen a male disciple to care for His mother after He was gone. Peter and the others certainly would have known this "other disciple whom Jesus loved." Mary would have also. Yet it almost seems the writer of the Gospel of John went to some length *not* to reveal the identity of this person. Why? Just before Jesus breathes His last breath upon the cross, He looks down at His mother and the disciple whom He loves and gives them both a final instruction:

> *When Jesus therefore saw his mother and the disciple standing by, whom he loved, he said to his mother, Woman, behold thy son. Then saith he to the disciple, Behold thy mother. And from that hour that disciple took her into his own home.*

> —JOHN 19:26–27

It is conceivable that, as many suggest, Jesus might have entrusted His mother, a widow, to John's care, especially since it is believed that Jesus was particularly close to this male disciple. But Mary Magdalene was financially independent, capable, intelligent, loving, and filled with the Holy Spirit, and she understood Jesus as none other. She knew His mother and, like a loving, devoted daughter, remained by her side, grieving with her while the men, fearing persecution, fled. If Jesus had instructed her to care for His mother, Mary would have (and may have) accepted that sacred role and done an incredible job. Some may argue that because Mary wasn't a son, Jesus' comment could not have referred to her. Yet, when He said, "Woman, behold your son," might He have been asking His mother to look up at Him for the instruction He then gave?

Ways to Invoke the Holy Blessings of Saint Mary Magdalene

Take a devotional walk. You could walk around your block, through your neighborhood, or to a park. Imagine you are Mary. Keep your mind focused on Jesus just as she would have done. Mentally repeat the words, "Jesus, you are my Lord and Savior," whispering it softly or silently in rhythmic cadence with your steps. Like Mary, let your mind, your lips, your heart, and your steps work together in adoration of Him.

Grow forget-me-not flowers, *myosotis sylvatica*. These plants bear tiny but profuse blue flowers in spring, heralding the end of the barren winter and suggesting the promise of seasons to come. Plant them in a pretty pot or in your spring garden in memory of Mary Magdalene and her love for Jesus.

Set aside a holy hour. Bow to the Lord in reverence. Pray for the gift of the Holy Spirit to unite your heart with Saint Mary Magdalene so that you may pray to the Lord with Mary's love. Be still. Slow your thoughts. Quiet your mind. Take a deep breath. Mentally praise, pray, contemplate, and receive. Be fully present to the Lord's presence.

Share your faith with a loved one or a friend. Turn off the television and talk. Get together for coffee or afternoon tea. Share your experience of living life with Christ as your savior. Engage in faith-sharing to strengthen your beliefs and remind you of the important role that faith plays in your life.

Affirmations

- ❧ *I am a child of God and, as such, am capable of accomplishing great things.*

- ❧ *Each day, I let go of imperfection and see others as though through Mary's eyes, seeing God's perfection in all.*

- ❧ *I make my appointment with God the most important meeting of my day.*

Prayer to Saint Mary Magdalene

OH BLESSED LADY, treasure of Jesus' heart, inspire me to turn inward to seek Him in that beautiful, quiet place where the distractions of the world cannot touch me. May the spark of my love ignite a fire that burns ever more brightly within my soul. May I feel the presence of the Holy Spirit baptizing and pulling me ever more deeply into the mystery of the Divine. May my soul rise, as if a bride on wings, to meet the Bridegroom in the temple of my heart. Saint Mary Magdalene, may the holy light that burns within me emanate outward to touch others in the world, as your light touches me now. Pray for me, Saint Mary Magdalene, that I shall discover how to be like you, a fully self-actualized, spiritual woman and powerful leader who loved Jesus as no other. I ask that you, in your capacity as Jesus' closest friend, carry my prayer on your heart to Him. Thank you, Saint Mary Magdalene, for hearing my petitions and interceding on my behalf to our Lord. Amen.

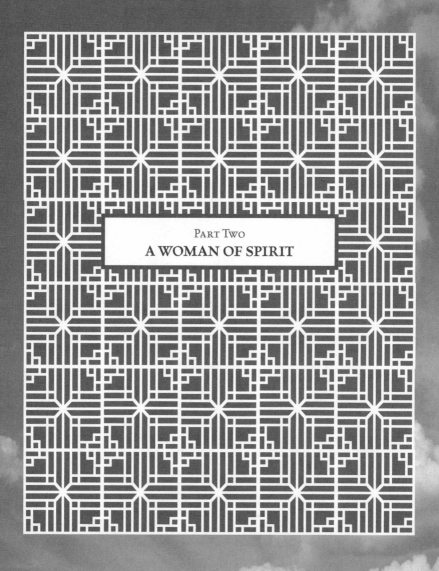

PART TWO

A WOMAN OF SPIRIT

CHAPTER 3

MARY MAGDALENE AS SPIRITUAL LEADER

With my whole heart have I sought thee: O let me not wander from thy commandments. Thy word have I hid in mine heart, that I might not sin against thee.

—PSALMS 119:10–11

*I*n the spiritual gatherings of modern women, an ancient sister's name— Mary Magdalene—often emerges. A perfect disciple, she served as a powerful spiritual leader for the women of her time, and she continues to be a role model for modern women as well. Though Mary lived long ago, she remains a light bearer and trailblazer for those of us who seek to bring divine grace, goodness, and light into our lives.

Jesus didn't just choose men for His ministry. He also sought women. Men and women have different temperaments and bring different gifts to discipleship and spiritual leadership. Mary Magdalene was someone with whom other women could closely relate. While devoting herself to Jesus and His work, she lived and traveled with His female followers. Maybe she helped find shelter and food. Perhaps she prepared meals with the other women, including the Passover meal now known as the Last Supper. And although on many occasions she may have been tired herself, she may still have washed and anointed Jesus' feet when He was exhausted from walking and preaching all day.

One mark of a great leader is never expecting someone else to do what you are not willing to do yourself. Jesus set the leadership example for all His followers, and Mary Magdalene followed His example. She would not have backed down from any leadership role required of her so long as it served her purpose—and her purpose was to serve Jesus.

She may not have expected that the work she was called to do would magnify her, but it did. To lead others to the Christian way, she could simply have been herself, doing the work inspired by those sayings of Jesus that may have taken hold of her heart and mind: "Love one another as I have loved you." "Blessed are the pure in heart for they will see God." "If you forgive others their transgressions, your heavenly father will forgive you." "Seek first the kingdom of God." "Do unto others as you would have them do unto you." These and so many other sayings of her teacher would have inspired and guided her.

Thinking of Jesus' loving words, Mary would have found it easy to speak gently, soothe suffering, minister to the sick and downtrodden, smile often to express God's joy, and encourage new followers to strengthen their faith. For herself, Mary Magdalene could have returned to Jesus' sayings throughout her life to find comfort, solace, strength, and wisdom. His words would have lifted her heart when she felt heavily burdened. They would have brought praise to her lips and called forth memories of Jesus' discourses. An aura of kindness and love surely emanated from this holy woman as she shared Jesus' teachings with those who yearned to know Him the way she knew Him.

Gifts of the Holy Spirit

No one really knows for certain what gifts the Holy Spirit may have bestowed upon Mary Magdalene after Jesus was crucified, but one thing is certain. She fully participated in the early communities of Jesus' followers. We know from the Gospel of Mary that she received sacred teachings in visions, and from legends we can decipher that she healed others through the will of God. It is also believed that she preached not only in her own community but, like many other believers in the Jesus movement, evangelized outside her own country, in places such as Gaul, for example, so she was certainly able to articulate the teachings of the Christ.

God blesses each of us differently and gives us the spiritual gifts He knows are right for us. Mary Magdalene was fortunate to be close to her teacher, and she received spiritual knowledge not given to others. She was the first to witness the Resurrection and to hear words from the risen Lord's lips. She was the first to receive His commission to go and tell the others. This honor of being the first to spread the good news of Jesus' resurrection and bring His message to the others—what some call the first act of preaching—was singularly Mary Magdalene's.

To this day, many Catholic churches all over the world are named in Mary Magdalene's honor. But you won't ever find a woman officiating or preaching a homily in any of them. That is because Pope Gelasius banned women from serving as priests in A.D. 494. More than a millennium later, this issue is still a point of contention between the Catholic Church's orthodox male leadership and forward-thinking men and women who believe the policy needs to change. Feminist theologians are sounding the rallying call

The Women Around Mary Magdalene

Mary Magdalene was in a core group of women who devoted themselves to Jesus and His work. They constantly traveled with Him, seeing to His needs.

Mary, mother of Jesus, was also called the Blessed Virgin Mary and *Theotokos*, Greek for God-bearer. She fulfilled an Old Testament prophecy that God would incarnate through a virgin birth. When the angel told her she was pregnant before she was married to Joseph, she accepted her mission with humility and dignity. She necessarily played a central role in Jesus' early life but is rarely mentioned in biblical accounts of His adult life. From earliest times, the Church has portrayed her as the embodiment of perfect womanhood, exemplifying merciful compassion, love, comfort, understanding, and forgiveness. She remained ever gracious and deeply committed to her son and His messianic mission.

Martha, the sister of Lazarus and Mary of Bethany, was mistress of the home she shared with her siblings. Martha was the one who bustled about getting meals ready while Mary Magdalene sat at Jesus' feet and anointed him with perfumed oil. When Lazarus died, Martha told Jesus that her brother would not have died if Jesus had not waited four days before arriving to heal him. After she made the remark, Jesus raised Lazarus from the dead.

Mary Jacobi, mother of James the Less and Joses, followed Jesus around Galilee and "contributed" to His work. The Bible's word "contributed" means providing financial support and other help. She, along with Mary Magdalene and other women, was involved in the events surrounding Jesus' death, burial, and resurrection.

Mary, a companion of Peter, was the mother of John Mark, the disciple to whom the Gospel of Mark is attributed. She may have been a well-to-do member of the Jerusalem church that Peter led after the death of Jesus. Her son John Mark is believed to have been the young disciple who fled from the scene of Jesus' arrest. Mary hosted a prayer session when Peter was released from his imprisonment.

Mary, wife of Clopas and possibly sister-in-law of Joseph, Jesus' earthly father, was one of three women the Scriptures cite as often traveling with Jesus (the others are his mother and Mary Magdalene). She was at the cross with Jesus' mother and Mary Magdalene.

Salome, mother of John and James and wife of Zebedee, followed Jesus from Galilee. She was also at the cross with the other women, albeit far off, and she went with them to anoint Jesus' body with perfumed oil, unguents, and spices.

for the orthodoxy to allow women to have the right to become ordained. They refer to Mary Magdalene, saying she was spiritually powerful in her own right and clearly ordained by Jesus. After Jesus' death, she was the first leader (and heir-apparent, some say).

Spiritual activists ask why women today cannot become priests and bishops in their community churches, pointing out that after Jesus' death, both women and men served as leaders. Women could preach, participate in religious discussions and decision-making, and form spiritual communities. The Gnostic Christians allowed women to help with baptisms and exorcisms as well. It probably wasn't Mary Magdalene's intention to bruise male egos deliberately; it's just that her holy mission played a primary role in her life.

Respected by Others

The best leaders know respect is not an entitlement; it is earned. Much of the current scholarship about Mary Magdalene in contemporary books says that it is likely she was a respected woman of some standing. It takes time to gain the respect of others, so she had probably served in leadership roles prior to joining Jesus' group of followers. Previous service as a leader is a good predictor of future leadership. But Mary had many traits other than those described in Chapter 1. As you'll see from what follows, she was likely a spiritually adept and gifted leader—perhaps someone whose talents, abilities, and light Jesus may have immediately recognized.

Self-Determined

Mary had another life before becoming Jesus' disciple, but she gave it up to follow Him. The Bible does not tell us exactly what she left behind; there is no mention of a family or children. Nor does it reveal how old she was when she met Jesus. During that first meeting, Jesus may have spoken to her in a way that opened her heart to His words. Whatever He said, His words must have resonated within her, because we know that she went against the social norms of the day, forsaking her old life (and family, if she had one) to join Him and the new, growing Christian family. Jesus had to ask the male disciples to follow Him, but He did not have to ask Mary. Her choice was made the moment she met Jesus.

Trustworthy

Mary would have been trustworthy. How else could she have become Jesus' closest friend and confidante? Jesus must have known He could count on her to keep secret the things He asked her not to reveal.

"It is to those [who are worthy of my] mysteries that I tell my mysteries."
—THE GOSPEL OF THOMAS II: 62, THE NAG HAMMADI LIBRARY

Jesus asked Mary and all others to believe in God and in Him, the Son of God. This was not difficult for Mary. She believed wholeheartedly and pledged Him her life in service and love.

Let not your heart be troubled: ye believe in God; believe also in me.
—JOHN 14:1

Responsible

Mary Magdalene stood vigil at the cross, taking full responsibility for her chosen path and beliefs. Under the watchful eyes of the Romans, the Pharisees (Jews of the Hasidic sect), and the Sadducee priests (who likely supported the Roman position to arrest Jesus), Mary Magdalene remained a testament to the love, faith, and loyalty she bore for Jesus. On that fateful day when He was crucified, that single act could have held dire consequences—she could even have been killed. But she did not desert Jesus, flee, or hide herself away in a secret place. She understood her role and knew how to read the moment.

> *They said to him, "Tell us who you are so that we may believe in you."*
>
> *He said to them, "You read the face of the sky and of the earth, but you have not recognized the one who is before you, and you do not know how to read this moment."*

—THE GOSPEL OF THOMAS II: 91, *THE NAG HAMMADI LIBRARY*

Spiritually Evolved

In order for Mary Magdalene to fulfill her role as a disciple, Jesus would have blessed her in ways to ensure that her spirit would grow in strength, truth, and light. He must have recognized something unique and special in her—a pure heart and perhaps wisdom beyond her years. She might have had strong intuition, the way so many women often do. Sometimes women can just look at a friend or family member and know something is wrong.

Perhaps Mary Magdalene knew (although, at the same time, she probably didn't want to admit it) that the hour had come for Jesus to lay down His life in fulfillment of the Old Testament prophecy.

Imagine the terrible feeling of dread she and Jesus' mother must have felt. Maybe the two women tried desperately to talk Him out of going in through the gates of Jerusalem that Passover weekend. Perhaps they tried to convince Him to keep out of sight. But Mary Magdalene's words, however tearful or persuasive they may have been, were futile. Yet, because she always followed Jesus' example, Mary Magdalene surely must have forgiven those who put Jesus—the person she loved above all others—to death. Somehow, Mary Magdalene found the strength to stand strong during this painful experience. She must have understood Jesus' supreme example of self-sacrifice, for she showed great moral courage in supporting Him to the end. Afterward, she comforted others and led them to a place of solace and peace. She understood that she, along with everyone who believed in Jesus and was willing to do the will of God, was now a member of His true family.

Then one said unto him, Behold, thy mother and thy brethren stand without, desiring to speak with thee.

But he answered and said unto him that told him, Who is my mother? And who are my brethren?

And he stretched forth his hand toward his disciples, and said, Behold my mother and my brethren!

—Matthew 12:47–49

There is a lot of speculation surrounding this holy woman. Some scholars have intimated that Mary Magdalene was not just Jesus' companion, partner, confidante, and consort (according to one theory) but also his spokesperson, the disciple he most loved, possibly the Beloved Disciple mentioned in the Gospel of John, and perhaps the author or primary source for that gospel. While scholarly theories abound and attempts are made to prove or disprove them, Mary Magdalene remains an inspiration and prime example of a spiritually evolved individual. With humility and love, she sowed the seeds of Christian faith throughout the places where she lived. As word of her holiness spread throughout the world, churches were erected in homage to her greatness.

Significance of the Anointing

The word *messiah* from the Hebrew *māshîach* means "the anointed." In one incident that foreshadows events to come, a woman (who some speculate was Mary Magdalene) breaks an alabaster jar of expensive spikenard (ointment) and pours it over Jesus' head. The scent must have permeated the whole house. Some of those present were upset by the woman's extravagance and complained that the spikenard could have been sold for more than 300 days' wages, money they could have used in the ministry. But Jesus told them to leave her alone.

. . . Why trouble ye the woman? For she hath wrought a good work on me.

For ye' have' the' poor always with you; but me' ye' have' not always.

For in that she' hath poure'd this ointment on my body, she' did it for my burial.

—Matthew 26:10–12

The anointing of Jesus by a woman generally accepted to have been Mary Magdalene has spiritual significance that the other disciples do not readily understand. Jesus must tell them that He will not always be with them. The time will soon come for His burial.

MARY MAGDALENE EMBODIED WISDOM

"The number seven was associated with Holy Spirit and with Holy Wisdom—the Sophia sought by philosophers, (literally, "lovers of wisdom") who, according to a first-century work called *The Wisdom of Solomon*, was described as 'the immaculate Mirror of God's energy' and 'spouse of God,'" writes Margaret Starbird in *Magdalene's Lost Legacy, Symbolic Numbers and the Sacred Union in Christianity*. Further, the author suggests that the correspondence of the goddess number with Mary Magdalene is crucial to the correct understanding of the gospel story. In long-standing tradition, it was Mary Magdalene, believed by early Gnostics to be an incarnation of the Sophia, who anointed Jesus at the banquet at Bethany—ritually proclaiming Him messiah, which literally means "the anointed one."

There is no question that Mary Magdalene played a leading lady's role in Jesus' story, but this statement is not meant to be disrespectful or to subtract anything from the Blessed Virgin Mary, Jesus' mother. Catholicism teaches that the Blessed Virgin was conceived without sin, unlike Mary Magdalene and the rest of us. Mary Magdalene, made whole by the compassion of Jesus, participated fully in the round-table discussions that Jesus had with the twelve chosen disciples. If Jesus believed only men should preach about the Kingdom of Heaven and serve as apostles, why did He choose Mary Magdalene to be the first to see His transcendent and eternal body and to proclaim the good news? Why, unless He knew of her mission as His spiritual leader on earth? Yet her role became more obscure through the centuries as orthodox bishops and popes enforced the conservative view of women, such as the ideas Paul expresses here in a letter to Timothy.

I will therefore that men pray everywhere, lifting up holy hands, without wrath and doubting.

In like manner also, that women adorn themselves in modest apparel, with shamefacedness and sobriety; not with broidered hair, or gold, or pearls, or costly array;

But (which becometh women professing godliness) with good works.

Let the woman learn in silence with all subjection.

But I suffer not a woman to teach, nor to usurp authority over the man, but to be in silence.

—1 TIMOTHY 2:8:12

THE SACRED NUMBER SEVEN

In the ancient world, seven stood for the "sacred feminine." Mary Magdalene has been called Sophia and goddess of the sacred feminine, counterpart to Jesus. The number seven has been called holy, mystical, and magical. It is a number meaning completion (of natural cycles, for example), fullness, and perfection.

The number seven is mentioned over 700 times in the Bible. Potently symbolic, it was a number often used by Jewish mystics and early Christians. God's day of rest is the seventh day of the week. Jesus spoke of the number seven in multiples, such as saying that when and how often one should forgive should number seventy times seven. The demons said to plague Mary Magdalene (which in her lifetime often meant illness) also numbered seven.

Mary Magdalene's Secret Teaching

The Gospel of Mary reveals a teaching that Mary received in a vision. When Peter asks her to share those things she remembers about Jesus but that His followers have not heard and therefore do not know, Mary says she will tell them what has been hidden from them. In a story that has three distinct parts, she shares the teaching she received in a vision.

Her Vision of Jesus

Mary Magdalene tells Andrew, Peter, and whoever else is present that she saw Jesus in a vision and that He praised her for not being afraid to see Him that way.

Ways to Invoke the Holy Blessings of Saint Mary Magdalene

Make a mask in honor of Mary Magdalene. Masks dramatically express symbolism. Find a plastic form in a craft store or make your own from casting material. Using a hot glue gun, cover the mask in fabric, decorative paper, beads, gold and red ribbon, lace, heavy cording, feathers, tiny bird eggs, found objects, silk flowers—whatever appeals to you. Add images of icons and an iconographic pattern. Whenever you gaze upon the mask, it should evoke within you feelings of admiration for the holiness and power of Mary Magdalene.

Cook some hard-boiled eggs in beet juice. Make red egg salad in honor of the legend of Mary Magdalene and the red egg. Think of how bold she must have been to share the story of the Crucifixion and Resurrection with the Emperor of Rome. Consider her desire to open his mind and heart to Christian beliefs. While you make the egg salad, ask for Saint Mary Magdalene to bless your heart with goodness, grace, and love so that the food may become holy. Have a tea party. Serve egg salad tea sandwiches to your guests along with inspiring words of faith.

Make a beautiful dream journal. Use exotic papers, beads, shells, silk ribbon, pressed flowers, and other elements that you think will make it "dreamy" and holy. Incubate a dream

Affirmations

➣ *I stand sentry at the door of my thoughts, blocking all negative thinking. I allow only positive, optimistic, constructive, and truthful thoughts to enter.*

➣ *Each day, I let go of imperfection. I see others as though looking through Mary Magdalene's eyes, seeing only God's perfect work in all.*

involving Mary. Before you go to sleep, mentally relax every part of your body. Take three cleansing breaths. Pray for Mary to come to you in your dream and bless you. If you'd like her help in finding a solution to a particular problem, ask for it. In the morning, write your dream in the dream journal. Interpret the dream using a dream symbol dictionary (there are many available). *Divining Your Dreams* by Jonathan Sharp (Fireside books, Lark Productions, LLC, 2002) draws meaning from the Kabbalah, the Jewish mystical tradition that is more than 4,000 years old. Probe for the dream's meaning, as Mary would—look beneath the surface of your dream to understand its mystery, symbolism, and underlying truth.

Read about the Kabbalah. Decipher its meaning in the context of those ancients who understood it to be secret teachings that God gave to Moses about the forces of creation and the relationship of humans with these forces. Kabbalists believe that all things are interconnected, so consider the connections that Mary Magdalene may have made in her life. How is your life as a Christian today connected to others, and in what ways do you work together as a spiritual community? A great book to read for reference is Kim Zetter's *Simple Kabbalah* (Conari Press, 2000).

Affirmations

&❧ I use my mind to create an imaginary space filled with the perfume of myrrh and light. Here is where I commune with Mary and our Lord, remembering His counsel that one's treasure is where the soul's mind is.

Means of Seeing Him

In her vision, she asked Jesus how it was she could see His body, and He told her that it was not through the soul or spirit but through the mind between the two. Jesus told her that where this "mind" is, there also is her treasure. Other authors have interpreted this mind as intuitive consciousness, a spiritual mind, and even a kind of super-conscious imagining. Then the story stops, because the next four pages of the Gospel of Mary are missing.

Rise of the Soul

When the story begins again, Mary Magdalene reveals the heart of the teaching. She explains that the soul, in its ascent to a place where it can rest in silence for eternity, passes through seven powers. They include the powers of darkness, desire, ignorance, death wish, fleshly kingdom, foolish fleshly wisdom, and wrath (or the angry person's wisdom).

Mary Magdalene's teaching seems to be about a mystical experience that the soul goes through to reach a place of rest. She describes the soul rising through seven centers, an idea that suggests an esoteric view of sacred energy or breath moving through force fields in the body. When the mind is calm and focusing on the upward rise of this energy, the soul witnesses it moving up the spine to the top of the head.

Mythologist Joseph Campbell, were he alive, might remind us of the story of Shakti, the divine feminine energy that ascends from the base of the spine to the head through seven force centers along the spine. Shakti pierces each center, releasing each center's gift, such as a heightened sense of hearing, smell, sight, psychic perception, etc. Once the energy pierces the seventh chakra, the ego (or sense of separateness from God) falls away, and the soul rests in a state of numinous transcendence and spiritual ecstasy.

Medieval mystics, including Hildegard of Bengin and Teresa of Avila, wrote of such experiences while in ecstatic states. Hildegard, whose spiritual gifts included writing music and creating artistic renderings of her visions, often used feminine symbolism as allegories for love, faith, wisdom, truth, and serene peace. After emerging from one of her ecstatic states, she would paint whatever she had seen. One of these "illuminations" was of Sophia, the goddess of divine wisdom, the same Sophia that some early Christian Gnostics believed Mary Magdalene to embody.

Reaction from the Apostles

In response to Mary's description of her vision, Andrew declared that he didn't think Jesus would say such things. Peter agreed. Mary wept and asked if they thought she had just fabricated the vision and lied about Jesus.

Be careful not to cause woman to weep, for God counts her tears. Israel was redeemed from Egypt on account of the virtue of its women.

—TALMUD

Matthew defended her and reminded the others that Jesus Himself found her worthy. Who were they to question Jesus' judgment? Peter and Andrew objected. They could not embrace the teaching. They did not understand it. Mary Magdalene, scholars assert, may have been the recipient of their jealousy and antagonism. But Mary Magdalene, because she had discovered how to transcend the sensory world of the flesh and enter the quieter realms of a more subtle soul consciousness, saw and heard Jesus. Mary attained *gnosis* (mystical knowledge).

In the Pistis Sophia, a Gnostic text, Mary shines as the chief questioner of Jesus during a discussion about Divine Wisdom's fall from the place of Light. Mary manages to ask eighty-five percent of all the questions. Author and scholar Susan Haskins writes in *Mary Magdalen, Myth and Metaphor* that when Mary Magdalene seeks permission from Jesus to speak boldly, Jesus' reply reveals that he holds her in high esteem. He generously praises her and tells her that He will reveal to her all the mysteries of the Divine because her heart yearns for knowledge of the such things more than the male disciples.

Through these examples, it is clear that Mary Magdalene was highly intelligent and hungered to know more. Having Jesus give her special attention, however, may have caused the male disciples to envy, doubt, threaten, confront, and devalue her. Perhaps they felt she monopolized their teacher's time. But Mary Magdalene was a good student who understood the lesson and soon moved on to the next level.

THE LEGEND OF THE RED EGG

After Jesus died, Mary Magdalene lived on, embracing Christian ideals. She evangelized (some say in Gaul and others suggest in Alexandria and Ephesus). At one point, legend has it, she tried to convert the emperor of Rome as they dined together. As she spoke about the Crucifixion and the Resurrection, the old monarch interrupted her, saying something like, "Madame, no more can a man rise from the dead than the white egg before us turn red." Mary picked up the egg, held it in the palm of her hand, and told him to watch. The egg instantly turned crimson.

The egg icon is found in art that features Mary Magdalene. One connection arises from the pagan festival named for Eostre, the Anglo-Saxon goddess of spring, which celebrates the end of dark winter and the start of spring. Pyansky eggs (the term comes from a Ukrainian verb meaning "to write upon") were hard-boiled and painted with colors rich in symbolism. Messages were written on some of the eggs. The tradition of making Pyansky eggs, which symbolized new hope, dates back to 4000 B.C. The symbol for the goddess Eostre was a rabbit. Subsequently, the colored eggs and rabbits that tied into the ancient pre-Christian celebration of spring and coincided with the time of the Resurrection became incorporated into the Christian celebration of Easter.

Some of the popular egg colors and their symbolism include black, things unknown and eternal; red, passion and happiness; yellow, fertility and wisdom; white, purity and sacredness; blue, truth and spirituality; and green, longevity and hope.

Hail Mary Magdalene, who, through enduring love and faithful companionship to our Lord, reflects the beauty, brilliance, and brightness of Heaven, hear my prayer. By your presence and proximity to the Eternal Son of God when He yet walked upon the Earth, you exhibited the qualities of spiritual discipleship for all to see and emulate. Teach me to be respectful that I might also be respected. Inspire me to be self-determined, responsible, and trustworthy. Help me find my way to the light that was your solace, to the presence of divine purity that you found cleansing, and to the comfort of Him, the remover of ignorance and delusion. O Mysterious Maiden, show me how to be a light bearer and perfect chalice for the sacred words of the Scripture. I ask that you bless my prayerful request with your love and carry it to our Lord, Jesus Christ. Thank you, most holy Mary Magdalene, for hearing my petition and for your intercession on my behalf. Amen.

Chapter 4

THE FIRST FEMALE APOSTLE

And again he said, Whereunto shall I liken the kingdom of God?
It is like leaven, which a woman took and hid in
three measures of meal, till the whole was leavened.

—Luke 13:20–21

Have you ever stopped to notice bread dough rising? Something magical happens when yeast, tepid water, and flour are mixed together and tucked away in a warm, draft-free spot. A powerful, unseen action causes the dough to rise. The ingredients and the environment are critical for successfully producing bread, but from a few simple ingredients, a wonderful new thing emerges. Similarly, Mary Magdalene, as leaven, served as a catalyst for the expansion and evolution of the early Christian church. If she had refused Jesus' directive on Easter morning and had not shared the news with her brethren that Jesus had risen from the dead, the church might have disintegrated.

Given the importance of her role as apostle to the apostles and her willingness to do all Jesus asked of her with compassion and grace, it is shocking that her contribution to Christianity's beginning could ever have been undermined. Yet it took only a century or two for the male leadership and power within the developing church to establish a hierarchy of men who could trace their authority back to the first disciples. These men would ultimately make all the rules that everyone else was expected to follow.

But what of the women whose spiritual lineage originated with Mary and Salome and the other female disciples of Jesus. Where were they—the would-be priestesses, bishops, and papesses? Why weren't these women who devoted themselves to Jesus, supported Him out of their own financial resources, and abandoned their previous lives to heed His call entitled to lead His church and minister to His flock? Didn't they yearn to work alongside their male counterparts to administer the holy sacraments of baptism, confirmation, the Eucharist, matrimony, penance, holy orders, and extreme unction? Hadn't Jesus set the example for them by commissioning a woman—Mary Magdalene—to be His apostle to the apostles? How greatly Jesus must have valued her. Yet, in time, Mary's reputation would be besmirched, accounts of her role in Christ's life diminished, and her personal story relegated to the fringes of historical accounts of Jesus and the birth of Christianity.

Mary Belonged in Jesus' World

In the hierarchy of importance in Mary Magdalene's world, men took the top position, followed by their beasts of burden. Women and children were important, but only in the context of belonging (like any other piece of property) to a man's family or tribe. Jesus clearly understood the plight of women. He sympathized with the yoke of oppression under which they lived and labored. For Mary Magdalene and her spiritual sisters—some of whom were ostracized from society because of illness, defects, and a gravity of sins—Jesus blew a soft breath of hope into their tedious lives. Both Jewish and Gentile alike, He forgave them, healed their broken bodies, saved them from being stoned to death, and restored their dignity. No wonder Mary and many others, even some who were married to Roman men, chose to follow this egalitarian teacher from Galilee. They left their worlds to be part of Jesus' world and eagerly became disciples. But while Jesus may have had egalitarian views toward women, He chose from a wide following of both men and women only twelve males to receive more advanced teachings.

In the first century, a double standard existed. Women belonged in the home, pounding grain into flour, cleaning fish, cooking meals, keeping house, and attending to the needs of their men or caring for their children. The men of Jesus' time must have thought He was out of His mind to expect the same standard of behavior and treatment would be afforded both sexes. But Jesus showed women—and men too—a visionary way to love all and to make their lives more meaningful by serving others and not judging one another.

Judge not, that ye be not judged.

—MATTHEW 7:1

This was the world of Mary Magdalene. She was a good and pious girl who observed the festivals and holy days of her religion. The Gospels and other early writings in the first century and later do not tell us about her

Fast Facts : Disciple Data

The twelve disciples lacked a higher education, but they did have a strong understanding of the history of their Hebrew faith and its doctrines. Because of their obtuse and dull comprehension, they tried Jesus' patience at times, and yet, scholars say, He showed restraint and tolerance toward them. Mary Magdalene was not one of the twelve, but she was considered a disciple because the term, in its broadest sense, describes any follower of Jesus who embraces His teachings and endeavors to conform to His principles. The Gnostic texts reveal that Mary held a lofty place in Jesus' inner circle and received advanced teachings.

Andrew was the first disciple called by Jesus. He and his brother Simon Peter were fishermen. Some stories say he preached in Scythia and was martyred in Achaia on an X-shaped cross (now referred to as Saint Andrew's cross).

Bartholomew was knowledgeable about the Hebrew Scriptures and may have been a native of Cana in Galilee. He is identified as Nathanael in the Gospel of John, but scholars say that may have been his surname. Legends say he evangelized in India, Asia Minor, and Armenia, where he was flayed and beheaded.

James the Less, son of Alphaeus, was brother to Matthew, the tax collector. Not much is known about him. He might have been beaten to death after the Sanhedrin sentenced him to be stoned.

James the Elder, son of Zebedee and Salome, was the older brother to John (who some believe was the Beloved Disciple). Herod Agrippa I ordered James executed, and James became the first apostle to be martyred for his Christian faith.

John, brother of James the Elder, was called the Evangelist, the Revealer, and the Beloved Disciple. Some scholars, however, suggest that Mary Magdalene may have been the Beloved Disciple and that she either wrote the Gospel of John or was the source for it.

Judas Iscariot was the disciples' treasurer. He became angry with Mary Magdalene for using an expensive spikenard to anoint Jesus' head. Later, Judas betrayed Jesus for thirty pieces of silver. Overcome with guilt, he hung himself. Matthias took his place as the twelfth disciple.

Matthew, son of Alphaeus, was a tax collector for the Romans. Also called Levi, meaning "gift of God," he wrote the Gospel of Matthew and may have been martyred in Ethiopia, although other accounts place him in Persia.

Philip, whose name in Greek means "he who loves horses," was the third disciple called. He came from Bethsaida, also Andrew's and Peter's hometown. Gnostic Christians held him in high regard, and he was the only apostle mentioned in the Gospel of Philip.

Simon the Cananean was a Zealot or Jewish patriot and a disciple of Jesus. Zealots believed violence was justified when it accomplished a good result (such as freedom from foreign oppression).

Simon Peter was Andrew's married brother. Jesus called him Cephas, meaning "rock." Peter and Andrew followed John the Baptist until they met Jesus. Peter led the Jerusalem church and was martyred on a cross, where he was hung upside down in deference to Jesus' crucifixion.

Thaddaeus, the son of James, is also known as Judas and is not to be confused with Judas Iscariot. The name Thaddaeus means "beloved." Little is known about him.

Thomas, sometimes called Judas Thomas, was the doubting Thomas of the scriptures and was also known as Didymus (twin).

physical attributes but infer much about her inquisitive mind and ability to articulate her thinking beautifully and clearly. Writers have called her magnificent, ethnically Jewish, an outspoken leader, an advocate for Jesus and His teachings, a diplomatic and effective missionary, the spiritual partner to Jesus, and a champion for women. Her family's wealth ensured that she did not have to worry about basic necessities. But Mary was not perfect. An illness of an extreme nature (some say epilepsy) tormented her until Jesus restored her to wholeness.

Jesus reserved for her a place in His inner circle and a special mission. If He had selected someone else, things might have turned out very differently for the fledgling Christian church. While the twelve disciples remained out of sight on that first Easter dawn, Mary gathered together her unguents and spices, determined to complete her act of love. She walked toward Jesus' tomb in the garden of Joseph of Arimathea. Joseph may have been Jesus' uncle and was certainly a follower of Jesus. He had arranged to have the body taken off the cross and carried to the sepulchre on his property. As Mary made her way toward the cave, her mind perhaps was filled with memories of happier times. Maybe she had been unable to sleep because her mind agonized over the horrific images of the man she loved being tortured to death. She may have wondered about His prophecy that if nonbelievers were to strike down His body, He would rise again after three days. With or without sleep, tortured or still in shock, Mary ventured forth into a morning landscape softly brushed by hues of predawn light.

She still carried a deep love for Jesus. His plan, in accord with the will of His Father, counted on that love. He could have revealed His transcendent form to any of His chosen twelve disciples or multitude of followers, but He chose Mary Magdalene. Might not Christians infer from Jesus' choice that He meant to show both genders were fit for leadership?

SACRED SYMBOLS FOUND IN MARY MAGDALENE'S WORLD

Beyond the egg that you read about in the previous chapter, other plants, animals, and foods are symbols that existed in Mary Magdalene's time, including the following:

Almond in Hebrew means "awakening." The almond tree welcomed spring to Palestine each year with pink and white blossoms symbolizing new life and the promise of hope. In the Old Testament, the rod that Aaron held forth (which sprouted buds and fruit and represented choosing God) was an almond branch.

Fig leaves covered Adam and Eve's nakedness. One of the first trees to be named in the book of Genesis, fig trees symbolized potency, safety, and prosperity. Ripe figs hang downward like eggs, representing new life. Jesus cursed a fig tree when he reached into its leaves for fruit and found it barren.

Fish symbolize spiritual renewal and rebirth as well as the Fisher of Men, a reverential title for Jesus. Fish also represent the subconscious mind charged by deep emotional or psychic currents.

Grapevines, grapes, and wine (made of fermented grapes) represent the spiritual life, transformation, and regeneration. Wine also means prosperity and the good life.

Palm fronds are an ancient triumphal symbol. The pagan god Apollo and the goddesses Ishtar and Astarte were associated with the palm motif. Christians celebrate Palm Sunday by waving palm fronds in their churches to honor the last time Jesus entered Jerusalem.

Olive trees symbolize victory, immortality, plenty, peace, and virginity. Victors and brides alike wore olive wreaths. When Noah released the dove from the ark and it flew back with an olive twig in its beak, it meant that God was giving humankind a sign of peace.

Mary Magdalene was the glue (or heir-apparent, according to one theory) that Jesus used to keep the fledgling Christian community from breaking apart after the Crucifixion and Resurrection. The disciples were unclear about their future and how to structure the movement. Some leaned toward men being in charge (after all, the twelve disciples were men), while others liked the gender-equal approach. They were uncertain exactly what constituted the "gospel" and how they were to carry it forward into other parts of the world. Who had the complete understanding of it and therefore the authority to teach it to others? Who could say with certainty that a particular person or persons correctly understood the path to salvation and could absolutely guarantee that those who followed them would receive it? Who could heal and exorcise demons or offer the sacraments?

According to biblical scholars, Mary Magdalene showed spiritual maturity, a bold determination, and fearlessness in her commitment to Jesus at the foot of the cross and at the tomb when He revealed Himself. Scholars say that her assignment from Jesus was incredibly important.

Jesus knew He could count on her to carry forth His words, and Mary did not falter.

> *And when they saw him, they worshipped him: but some doubted.*
>
> *And Jesus came and spake unto them, saying, All power is given unto me in heaven and in earth.*
>
> *Go ye therefore, and teach all nations, baptizing them in the Father, and of the Son, and of the Holy Ghost;*
>
> *Teaching them to observe all things whatsoever I have commanded you: and, lo, I am with you always, even unto the end of the world.*
>
> —MATTHEW 28:17–20

Jesus' Treatment of Women

Jesus encouraged women to follow Him. He accepted their acts of generosity and kindness, and He allowed them to financially support Him and His growing community. He allowed women to anoint Him, declaring after His anointing by Mary Magdalene that the world would recall that act in memory of her. Jesus revealed His identity as the Messiah to the Samaritan woman at the well in the Gospel of John. He took pity on a widow and raised her son from the dead, cured the hemorrhaging woman, restored Jarius' daughter, saved a women from a death by stoning, and healed Peter's mother-in-law and others. After His resurrection, the women followers of Christ banded together and joined other disciples for fellowship and prayer. Some sources say that women participated in the selection of Matthias to replace Judas. These women, on the day of

Ways to Invoke the Holy Blessings of Saint Mary Magdalene

Purchase a crystal chalice for your altar. It doesn't have to cost a fortune—you might find a small crystal bowl at a garage sale, in a friend's cupboard, or at a church flea market. Each day, fill it with life-giving water and float a freshly picked rose or another fragrant flower. Avoid handling or sniffing the flower, saving its gifts of beauty and scent for Jesus. Imagine you are Mary offering a symbolic gift of love as the first act of your devotion.

Make a poster of Mary Magdalene's discipleship. Draw seven boxes or circles on a sheet of paper. Number each of the boxes. Drawing upon the canonical gospels and facts you may learn elsewhere about Mary, write an important moment in her life in each box or circle. Using art images of Mary as well as symbols and other images or elements that you find, cut, paste, and create seven small collages in each box. For example, the first box could show Jesus healing her, the second could show her anointing Jesus, the third might reveal Mary praying with other women, the fourth might depict Mary at the foot of the cross, the fifth could show her at the empty tomb, the sixth might illustrate Mary seeing the risen Christ, and the seventh could show her evangelizing after Jesus' death. Through this artistic endeavor, you will learn more about this holy woman whom Jesus loved, someone He knew would

Affirmations

- *I add my voice to the female chorus, from Mary Magdalene to modern women, who fervently desire to proclaim the Lord's message of salvation.*

- *Each day I will cultivate the leadership qualities of Mary Magdalene, Apostle to the Apostles.*

faithfully carry out the job of apostle to the apostles.

Look up vesica piscis in your dictionary or encyclopedia. You will discover that it is an emblem, or mandorla, of Christ inside an upright almond shape. Study the symbol. Ask yourself why artists would portray Jesus within this shape. Offer a prayer and use this image as a departure point for contemplation.

Make an embossed vesica piscis. Purchase a medium-weight metal embossing sheet such as copper, silver, or gold (found in arts and crafts stores). These sheets come in inexpensive kits with a stylus. Because Mary Magdalene so deeply loved Jesus, choose an art image of him (rather than her) that you like and make a photocopy of it to use as a template. Cut the metal with scissors to a size slightly larger than the image area. Tape the template over the foil. Put the foil on top of a rubber mat or soft surface. Use the stylus to trace the image on top of the metal. When finished, decorate a mat or frame for your art with a pretty iconographic pattern (copies can be found in pattern books in libraries or bookstores). The pattern is best traced using a pen with gold ink. Hang the artwork in a place where you pray or like to be reminded of Jesus and His holy saints, especially Mary Magdalene.

Affirmations

❧ *When I perceive gender injustice, I will voice my concern and speak as Mary Magdalene did, with the power and grace and authority given to women by Jesus.*

Pentecost, received the gifts of the Holy Spirit and were filled with its power right along with the men. Female followers of Christ prophesied, preached, and prayed at church meetings. They managed to fully participate in this new community, though with some care so as not to usurp male authority and power.

Who Could Be an Apostle?

With the authority and power that God had invested in Him, Jesus conveyed the same authority and power to His twelve chosen disciples. The number twelve is notable because there were twelve tribes of Israel, the children of God. Jesus turned His devoted students or disciples into apostles and sent them forth to spread His message of salvation and life everlasting. The apostles met several criteria: They were taught by Jesus, witnessed His resurrected form (a lot of emphasis is placed on this), and were endowed with a commission to go forth and teach all nations. They were thusly empowered to heal, exorcise demons, and perform miracles.

When Judas Iscariot betrayed Jesus and subsequently committed suicide, the group of male apostles was reduced to eleven. They decided to replace Judas with Matthias. Later, after the Ascension, Paul also became an apostle. Paul was not in the core group that had been with Jesus from the beginning, but he met Jesus after the Resurrection. Paul, in his letter to the Corinthians, said of his meeting with Christ that Paul was one "born out of time."

And that he [the Savior] was seen of Cephas [Peter], then of the twelve:

After that, he was seen of above five hundred brethren at once; of whom the greater part remain unto this present, but some are fallen asleep.

After that, he was seen of James; then of all the apostles.

And last of all he was seen of me also, as of one born out of due time.

—I CORINTHIANS 15:5–8

The Thirteenth Apostle

Mary Magdalene, of course, met all the same criteria that the core group of twelve met to be apostles. In fact, she was the first among the disciples to fulfill one of the preeminent criteria—witnessing Jesus' resurrected body. Even Paul mentions this in his letter to the Corinthians:

Am I not an apostle? Am I not free? Have I not seen Jesus Christ our Lord?

—I CORINTHIANS 9:1

The Gnostics called Mary Magdalene the Thirteenth Apostle. In the Pistis Sophia, she is referred to as Apostle to the Apostles. She believed in and experienced the power of prophetic visions, which was a point of contention with Peter, who doubted the validity and truth of her visions. Clearly, all was not harmonious within Jesus' apostolic family. Rivalry, hotheadedness, and misogynist attitudes toward Mary became challenging issues for her. The Gnostic texts reveal that Peter bullied Mary Magdalene both before and after Jesus was crucified. While Jesus was still present in

His human body, He reprimanded Peter for such behavior toward Mary Magdalene. He knew that Peter was given to emotional outbursts and often spoke without considering the consequences. Still, Jesus corrected and forgave His disciple. Mary Magdalene also spoke up when Peter accused her of something, but it is likely that she too forgave him.

Jesus told His apostles neither to establish any law other than what He had given them nor to promulgate laws since, by doing so, they would risk being enslaved by the very laws they created. In the visionary teaching that Mary Magdalene revealed after she'd seen Jesus at the tomb, she spoke about the power of those who practiced deception in order to dominate. But the soul, knowing the truth, would defy the domination of deceitful laws made by powerful people and would thus escape. The soul must make its way through a wrathful and wicked minefield in its quest to move toward the divine, Mary said. In the same way that Mary Magdalene described her inward journey, she could have been describing her outward journey as well. The main obstacles constraining her efforts to do Jesus' work in those turbulent times were those followers who did not believe it was appropriate for women to fulfill leadership roles in the religious community of early Christianity.

The early Christian sects grappled with this question. There were those who believed that patriarchal authority of the kind already in practice by the Jews and Romans ensured continuity. Other sects, like the Gnostics, felt that the sharing of power between men and women heralded a new and better way of sustaining and growing the Jesus movement. Yet even the Gnostics disagreed with one another. How did those closest to Jesus work through their differences to obtain conflict resolution? Mary, as the chief female disciple, must have had to step gingerly through the minefield of male posturing and rivalry, looking to Jesus for answers. What about her life after His death? Would she have assertively preached the gospel of salvation? Or would she have submitted to the male hierarchical order, retreated into a contemplative life, and focused on her own inner spiritual journey?

SYMBOLISM AND USES OF THE NUMBER TWELVE

Twelve was the number of apostles Jesus chose to spread the gospel to all nations. There are twelve months in the year, and day and night divide equally into two twelve-hour periods. Twelve stars sparkle in the crown of Mary, Queen of Heaven, and twelve is also the number of gods who commanded power and control over Olympus.

Scholars say there is evidence that Mary Magdalene did both: She evangelized for a while, and at some point she became a contemplative. The important point is that Mary Magdalene evaluated options, listened to her own heart, and figured out how she was going to live her life, rather than let herself be told how her life would have to unfold. At some point, she may have realized that patience, tolerance, and the right understanding of scripture and the law would be her best weapons for battling those dark powers of wrath and injustice and domination. She chose to live life as a devoted follower of Jesus. Through her leadership and preaching skills, she led others to that life as well.

Mary's Model for Perfect Leadership

Author Karen L. King asserts in *The Gospel of Mary of Magdala, Jesus and the First Woman Apostle* that "according to the master story, the full doctrine of Christianity was fixed by Jesus and passed on in the doctrines of the Church. The Gospel of Mary instead suggests that the story of the gospel is unfinished. Christian doctrine and practice are not fixed dogmas that one can only accept or reject; rather Christians are required to step into the story and work together to shape the meaning of the gospel in their own time."

Most important for Mary Magdalene and the first apostles, as well as for Christians today, is that Jesus himself practiced what He preached. He was, is, and always will be the perfect model for spiritual leadership.

Seeds of Discord

Historians point to the Gnostics as one of the early Christian sects that contributed to creating discord. The Gnostics' equal treatment of women became a source of friction for those like Peter and his brother Andrew, who espoused traditional or lesser roles for women while their own gender secured them higher status. Some feminist religious historians have suggested that the discord experienced by Jesus' inner circle may have come about through Peter's and Andrew's misunderstanding of Jesus' teaching. Peter viewed Mary Magdalene as just a woman, not a spiritually adept leader, and certainly not someone with authority equal to his and that of other males.

Other historians point out that the women around Jesus, especially Mary Magdalene, served Jesus with love, loyalty, and a deep, abiding commitment, even when it meant risking persecution and death. In contrast, among the men in Jesus' inner circle, one denied him (Peter), one doubted him (Thomas), and one betrayed him (Judas).

While many of the Gnostics viewed women as capable of preaching and performing tasks associated with the Church's teachings, Tertullian, a church leader who lived between the second and third centuries following the death of Jesus, stated unequivocally that it was unacceptable for women to offer the Eucharist, to speak or to teach within the church, to baptize, or to usurp any activity belonging to a male priest.

We are led to believe by feminist theologians and historians that Mary Magdalene and other early female followers of Jesus were pushed to the margins of the story of Christianity because of their gender—their bodies. Yet Jesus taught His followers not to place too much importance on their bodies.

. . . Therefore I say unto you, Take no thought for your life, what ye shall eat; neither for the body, what ye shall put on.

The life is more than meat, and the body is more than raiment.

—LUKE 12:22–23

The body is temporal, but the soul is eternal. The orthodox during Jesus' time believed that sin is what keeps humanity enslaved in physical and mental suffering and separate from God. The power to forgive humanity and grant salvation belongs to Jesus.

Many of the Gnostics, however, believed that it was not sin but ignorance that caused humans to suffer and that salvation could come only through self-knowledge—something that happens as a result of interior work rather than through the power of another. They also believed it was wrong to equate the body with one's true self. Mary Magdalene may have grasped the meaning behind these teachings, understanding that what Jesus taught was the Word of God, and the way He both taught it and lived it was what she chose to emulate.

Marriage or Celibacy?

It is widely believed that Mary Magdalene never married, but it is also speculated (especially in light of the translations of the Gnostic gospels and the associated commentary) that she may have been Jesus' wife. While there are no facts or historical documents to say that she was, it is widely accepted that Jesus was the great love of her life and remained so even after His death on the cross. Yet she could have married. Other apostles were married. Peter (Cephas) did not divorce his wife and abandon his family when he became a disciple. When his mother-in-law was ill with fever, Jesus went to her to heal her. Paul mentions Peter's marital status in a letter to the Corinthians.

Have we not power to lead about a sister, a wife, as well as other apostles, and as the brethren of the Lord, and Cephas?

—1 CORINTHIANS 9:5

That passage suggests that Peter was not the only apostle with a wife. The issue of marriage versus the single life and celibacy, if not discussed by the apostles, certainly would have been discussed in successive generations. Somewhere down the line of apostolic succession, it was decided that the power and authority of the Church belonged to celibate men and that those chosen would have to conform to an established order of hierarchy. These successors to the apostles were designated spirit-endowed men favored with infallible powers. Feminist scholars point out the irony that the rock upon which Jesus built his Church was not a celibate male but rather Peter, a householder.

In addition, the epistles reveal references indicating bishops and priests of the early Church were married. Also, during the first dozen or so centuries A.D., thirty-nine popes were married, and of them, three—Anastasius I, Sergius III, and Saint Hormidas—sired sons who achieved sainthood. Yet Pope Urban II in 1095 declared that those seeking ordination into the priesthood could not be married. It may be surprising for some to learn that Pope John Paul II made special exemption for married Protestant ministers who convert to Catholicism. Without having to abandon wives and children, they can be ordained into the priesthood and carry on as members of their families.

The leadership role of women in the Church during Mary Magdalene's lifetime and for centuries afterward became a flash point for heated debate. Every pope in the line of succession from Peter has probably given thought to the roles of women in the secular and religious worlds. Pope John Paul II, a popular leader who lived a transparent and exemplary life, was quite vocal about advocating for human rights, yet modern women face some of the same rivalry, threats, subjugation, and lack of rights that women experienced while Jesus was alive. Still, Mary Magdalene dedicated her life to Him and, because of Jesus, had some powerful weapons in her arsenal against domination: blessings of the Holy Spirit and Jesus' words and love.

And call no man your father upon earth: for one is your Father, which is in heaven.

Neither be ye called masters: for one is your Master, even Christ.

But he that is greatest among you shall be your servant.

And whosoever shall exalt himself shall be abased; and he that shall humble himself shall be exalted.

—MATTHEW 23:9–12

BLESSED SAINT MARY MAGDALENE, Apostle to the Apostles, hear my prayer. Inspire me to seek always the truth and not be duped into conforming to the status quo simply because it is easier than standing up for what Jesus believed. You, who lived an exemplary life after the Lord's healing touch, help me to hold a vision for inclusiveness and for healing the rifts between men and women in the world today. Guide my thoughts to right thinking about how to overcome adversity, tyranny, hate, racism, sexism, and xenophobia. Like you, may I become an example of a loving leader and spokesperson for the Savior on earth, showing others how to resolve conflict through beauty, love, grace, intelligence, and bold leadership. Most glorious Saint Mary Magdalene, I pray that you will favor me by carrying my prayer in your heart to our beloved Christ, most blessed of all leaders. Dearest Saint Mary Magdalene, thank you for your intercession on my behalf. Amen.

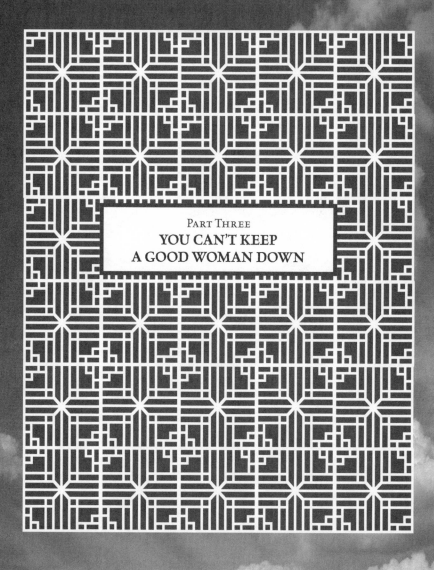

PART THREE

YOU CAN'T KEEP
A GOOD WOMAN DOWN

CHAPTER 5

WRITTEN OFF, WRITTEN OUT, AND THEN REVISED

And he' [Peter] said unto him [Jesus], Lord, I am ready
to go with thee', both into prison, and to death.
And he' said, I tell thee', Peter, the' cock shall not crow this day,
before' that thou shalt thrice' deny that thou knowest me'.

—LUKE 22:33–34

Have you ever fibbed about something only to regret it later? Did you feel guilty about lying? Have you ever had to tell a second or third lie to cover up the first? How did the deception make you feel?

There's no evidence to show that Mary Magdalene ever deceived anyone about being one of Jesus' followers. However, the New Testament Gospels say that Peter did. As Peter and Jesus walked toward the Mount of Olives after the Last Supper, Peter told Jesus he would never deny Him, even if everyone else did. But Jesus predicted Peter would not keep his word.

In the Garden of Gethsemane, Jesus asked Peter to maintain a vigilant watch while He prayed. Peter probably intended to do Jesus' bidding, but he fell asleep (perhaps because of the meal he'd just eaten or because he was tired). When Jesus finished praying and turned to find Peter sleeping, He must have been deeply disappointed.

. . . Simon [Peter], sleepest thou? Couldest thou not watch one hour?

—Mark 14:37

Later, after the soldiers had arrested Jesus, Peter fled into the night. When he again felt courageous, he accompanied John, another disciple, to the courtyard of the high priest where he mingled with servants. Perhaps sensing their enmity toward him when they asked him if he knew Jesus, Peter lied three times, saying he was not a follower and did not know that man.

On the other hand, Mary Magdalene did not lie about knowing Jesus. In fact, she openly proclaimed her commitment to Him by standing vigil at His cross where the Roman authorities, high priest, chief priests, elders, scribes, and others who had condemned Jesus could see her. There is nothing recorded in the canonical gospels about her ever fibbing about Jesus, lying to Him, or letting Him down. Regardless of her sterling example of devotion, however, Mary Magdalene's story was relegated to the margins of the New Testament Gospels. Biblical accounts of her role in Jesus' life and in the formation of the Church were minimized. Why was she mentioned at all? For one thing, she was too important to be completely ignored.

The gospel writers could have revealed so much more about Mary Magdalene, but their stories focus on the contributions of males to Jesus' life and ministry and to the origins of Christianity. Some of the apostles and men involved with the early Church during its first few centuries probably felt some gender bias toward Mary Magdalene, but this is something they would not have learned from Jesus. He never treated Mary Magdalene or any woman among His followers as inferior to His male disciples.

Men of that time may have thought Jesus crazy. Egalitarian treatment of women certainly stood in opposition to traditional patterns of thought and behavior in first-century Palestinian Jewish society. Most of the male disciples were raised to believe that women were intrinsically inferior. A man defined a woman's life, not the other way around. Subsequent generations of bishops and popes espoused the same beliefs.

Maybe, because Mary Magdalene was a woman with money and a message, some viewed her as upsetting the status quo. Perhaps they made her life more difficult. For her evangelical activities, she, like other disciples, risked persecution from Jews and Gentiles alike. But where her faith in Jesus was concerned, Mary Magdalene remained fearless.

After the Easter events, Mary Magdalene's story is dropped by the writers of the canonical gospels. She may have left Jerusalem in the company of other women followers in order to return to Galilee. Jesus' appearing to her on Easter morning surely must have inspired her and strengthened her faith. Perhaps she made a holy pledge to continue His work for the rest of her life. Undoubtedly, she felt compelled to evangelize. Why else would her popularity surge during that first century, as scholars say it did? Why else would so many legends about her survive for more than 2,000 years? If she'd just joined women in private homes for refreshments and to talk about the old times and to pray, wouldn't she have remained an obscure character in Christian history? Instead, she has evolved into a saintly model of inspiration to men and women for all time.

As for Peter, he returned to Galilee after the Crucifixion and suggested to his companions that they take up fishing again. Peter might have slipped back into his old, familiar life if it were not for a repeat of Jesus' miracle causing a bountiful catch of fish. Peter again turned his thoughts to Jesus. It was around that time, religious scholars say, that Peter took responsibility for leading Jesus' flock.

A Power Struggle Ensues

Schisms actually began among the early Christians soon after Jesus' death. Undoubtedly there were followers who rallied behind Mary Magdalene, asserting that she was Jesus' confidante, understood His teachings better than the other disciples, was qualified to be His spokesperson, and had a temperament well suited to leadership. In addition, she stood as a pillar of strength and calm under pressure (such as during Jesus' crucifixion and death).

Life wouldn't have been easy for Mary Magdalene, or any Jewish woman. During menstruation and after childbirth, women were considered unclean and were required to participate in a ritual cleansing (religious bath) to regain purity. They were not allowed to converse in public places with men they did not know. Some sources even state that women and men could not eat a meal together in their own homes. Even at the Last Supper, women served the men. The Gospel of Matthew reveals an incident involving Peter's mother-in-law that illustrates how a woman, even when she was recovering from an illness, had to get up from her sick bed and serve men's needs.

And when Jesus was come into Peter's house, he saw his wife's mother laid, and sick of a fever.

And he touched her hand, and the fever left her: and she arose, and ministered unto them.

—MATTHEW 8:14–15

Jesus may have set the example for better treatment of women, but it may have been too radical for His apostles. Clues to how Mary Magdalene and the other women around Jesus may have been treated can be found in the apostle Paul's letters to the Greek church of Corinth.

Let your women keep silence in the churches: for it is not permitted unto them to speak; but they are commanded to be under obedience, as also saith the law.

And if they will learn anything, let them ask their husbands at home: for it is a shame for women to speak in the church.

—I CORINTHIANS 14:34–35

After Jesus' death, women followers joined the men in acts of fellowship and prayer and, according to some sources, helped to elect Matthias. On the day of Pentecost, women as well as men received the power and gifts of the Holy Spirit. Mary Magdalene and her Christian sisters prayed and prophesied at church meetings in homes, but they were not allowed to usurp male leadership in public worship or exercise any kind of authority over their male counterparts. In spite of this, Christian women and slaves converted other women to follow Jesus' teachings.

Ways to Invoke the Holy Blessings of Saint Mary Magdalene

Make a T-shirt that declares your faith. Create an image of Mary Magdalene using oils, watercolor, or pen and ink. Or find an image you like—perhaps a holy card or a picture of her from an old religious magazine or calendar. Take the image to a copy center where workers can copy it onto heat-set transfer paper. Then, using a hot iron and following the instructions with the transfer, iron the image onto a T-shirt. Using the same technique, add a typed message, prayer, statement, or affirmation.

Read the Gospel of John and, everywhere the Beloved Disciple appears, substitute the name of Mary Magdalene. In instances when both Mary Magdalene and the Beloved Disciple are present together, ask yourself if it makes sense that her presence posed a problem for the revisionist and that perhaps to get around it the author added both names. Or is the theory of the Beloved Disciple's identity being that of Mary Magdalene absurd? Take time to read the gospel and ponder these questions.

Affirmations

❧ *I will not worry about the opinions of others. I know, as Saint Mary Magdalene knew, that only the Savior's opinion counts.*

Set aside a period for the adoration of Saint Mary Magdalene. Place a pretty cloth over a table that will serve as an altar. Set upon the table a picture of Mary Magdalene (gaze upon it), candles (light them to "bring the light" of truth and discernment), anointing oil (make the sign of the cross on your forehead with the oil), a beautiful flower (float it in a bowl as a symbol of your love and devotion), and a small glass of water (to be energized by your prayers and her blessings and to be consumed after the hour is over).

Make a pilgrimage to the National Galley of Art in Washington, D.C. As mentioned in the box that appeared earlier in this chapter, here you can view several preeminent paintings of Mary Magdalene.

Affirmations

- *As I go through my day, I will remember how Saint Mary Magdalene served Jesus in thought, word, and deed, and I will try to emulate her example.*

- *I will pray more fervently, not for my own self, but for the need of others.*

For some early Christian congregations, Mary Magdalene and her sisters in the faith served as teachers, leaders, and prophets in home churches and community gatherings. As their numbers grew stronger, perhaps their unity, power, and authority strengthened as well. Why else would someone like Timothy, associate of the apostle Paul, speak out so venomously against them unless they were somehow challenging male authority?

Let the woman learn in silence with all subjection.

But I suffer not a woman to teach, nor to usurp authority over the man, but to be in silence. For Adam was first formed, then Eve.

And Adam was not deceived, but the woman being deceived was in the transgression.

—I Timothy 2:11–14

Tensions Mount

Early Christians grew deeply divided over important issues—not just women's roles in religious service, but also the Church's direction and core beliefs. Even so, while dealing with these many problems, early Christians tried to find their way toward cohesiveness. The following are some of the obstacles they faced.

Persecution

Peter faced the challenges of evangelizing in Jerusalem, where he risked persecution and death. In fact, all Christians of the first century faced this threat.

Confusion

Paul wrote letters to the Corinthians to avert a splintering off of different factions within that community. For whatever reason, various members engaged in religious prostitution, temple sacrifices, and discrimination against the poor. Corinth was a city of moral depravity, and it was to Paul's credit that he exerted influence over the Jews initially. But it wasn't long before they turned against him. In his letters, Paul wrote confidently, with the power and authority of an apostle. He had to answer their questions, address their liturgical issues, and deal with their problems using an authoritative yet loving Christian approach. In one instance, he offered to take matters into his own hands (meet the troublemakers) if necessary.

Loyalty and Leadership

In the early days of Christianity, conflicts arose over who should lead the Church. Some early Christians claimed a loyalty to Peter, others were devoted to Mary Magdalene, and some were attached to Paul. Challenges were made to Paul's right to call himself an apostle. Paul had to fight false apostles for control of the young Corinthian church. Paul's followers believed he should be the authority for their church. Others defended Peter's right to be the church's founding father and its leader.

Vision

Who possessed a clear vision for what the Church was and what it would become? The early Christians met in private homes and other meeting places, but they did not initially set about erecting churches. As preachers evangelized from one town to the next throughout the Holy Land and even into other countries, the group of Jesus' followers grew larger and more culturally and ethnically diverse. Inherent in the growth of the movement were issues over who was in charge, how the movement would continue to grow, who could officiate and oversee new spiritual communities, who had final say over interpretations of Jesus' teachings, what the hierarchy of power would be, and what, if any, leadership roles women and slaves could fulfill. Some scholars suggest it was a time of uncertainty as Christians began to assess what worked, what didn't, and why.

Structure

Would the church structure take the form of a male hierarchy (a model already familiar to the early Christians), or would men and women share power?

Squabbling, power struggles, conflicts between individuals, and arguments over the roles of women added to the confusion and dissent. As the early Christians tried to live by Jesus' principles and establish communities of faithful people, it may have become obvious that they needed to write down Jesus' teachings as well as their own beliefs and stories.

WHAT ARE THE CANONICAL GOSPELS?

One way for the apostles to establish an authoritative and official account of their time with Jesus and their understanding of His message of salvation was to write a gospel. The Gospels are memoirs that include important tenets of the Christian faith. They are not biographies but may contain biographical elements. They do not include all the facts of Jesus' life or His ministry, but they do narrate important events and messages. They are not sermons per se, but they may feature preaching and discourses. They are used as instructional texts for believers.

Three of the four New Testament Gospels—Matthew, Mark, and Luke—are so similar in content and point of view that they are commonly referred to as the Synoptic Gospels. The fourth, the Gospel of John, differs from the other three in that it provides a theological view of Jesus' life, discusses His work in Judea rather than Galilee, and narrates different events from those in the other three gospels. All four are called canonical gospels because they conform to the canon (established rules, laws, and beliefs set forth by the Church).

Did Mary Magdalene Write the Gospel of John?

The authorship of the fourth gospel—the Gospel of John—is disputed. Many people believe that one of John's followers wrote it sometime between A.D. 90 and 110. In fact, Irenaeus, an early Church father, claimed that John, son of Zebedee, was the author of the fourth gospel. Irenaeus got his information from his childhood teacher Polycarp, bishop of Smyrna.

John was a fisherman who plied his trade around the Lake of Genesareth with his older brother James the Greater and his father. He and his brother were followers of John the Baptist until Jesus called them to become disciples.

Among the disciples, John figured prominently—some say even Peter took a secondary position to him. John was present on a number of momentous occasions: at the time Jesus raised Jairus' daughter, at the Transfiguration, in the Garden of Gethsemane, and during preparations for the Last

Supper, among others. Many believe that at the Last Supper, John was the Beloved Disciple who leaned against Jesus' chest.

During the Last Supper, Peter requested that the Beloved Disciple ask Jesus (instead of Peter asking himself) to reveal His betrayer's identity. Clearly, the Beloved Disciple and Jesus shared a special relationship, and it seems that whenever this disciple was around, Peter receded into the background. According to the fourth gospel, when Mary Magdalene proclaimed the tomb empty, Peter and "the other disciple whom Jesus loved" ran to see for themselves, but the "other disciple" outran Peter. When Peter went inside the tomb, the "other disciple" who "believed" followed him. Then, the text says, the disciples went home, leaving Mary standing outside the tomb, weeping.

If John or one of his followers wrote the fourth gospel, it may have been completed and later lengthened. There is a growing consensus that this gospel was not written by one person. For one thing, chapter twenty-one (the epilogue) is stylistically quite different from the rest, and biblical scholars believe it may have been added at a later time. Specific and accurate details not included in the other three gospels are also found in the Gospel of John, suggesting an eyewitness account. As a result, while tradition holds that the writer was John, there are biblical scholars who do not believe the evidence supports such a conclusion.

A newer theory based on a variety of reasons is that Mary Magdalene was either the writer or the eyewitness source for the gospel. Being ethnically Jewish, Mary Magdalene would have possessed great familiarity with Jewish custom and the Old Testament, and this was true of the writer of the fourth gospel. The author clearly had been an eyewitness to many of the events involving Jesus, as indicated by the many factual details presented about the Crucifixion, the wedding at Cana, the death and burial of Jesus, and the fish and loaves story, as well as the miraculous catch of fish on the Sea of Tiberias when Peter did not recognize Jesus but the Beloved Disciple did. And unlike the other three gospels, this gospel is symbolic and highly literary. The writer was aware that Jesus worked in a ministry of baptizing before he changed to a ministry of signs and preaching. The gospel itself proclaims its authorship.

> *Then Peter, turning about, seeth the disciple whom Jesus loved following; which also leaned on his breast at supper, and said, Lord, which is he that betrayeth thee?*
>
> *... This is the disciple which testifieth of these things, and wrote these things: and we know that his testimony is true.*
>
> —JOHN 21:20 AND 24

In this quote, the unnamed Beloved Disciple—the one whom Jesus loved and the same one who leaned on Jesus' chest at the Last Supper—is identified as the author of the Gospel of John. Biblical scholar Elaine Pagels, however, in her book *Beyond Belief*, is one of those scholars who asserts that the author of the Gospel of John may not have been John, son of Zebedee, as people generally believe.

> *Yet the gospel itself (and its possibly added conclusion) declares it was written by "the disciple whom Jesus loved." If John, the son of Zebedee was that "beloved disciple," why does his name never appear in the gospel, and why does the gospel never mention either "the apostles" or "the twelve"? If the*

author had been one of them, why doesn't he say so? Why, while acknowledging Peter as leader, does he simultaneously denigrate Peter's leadership in favor of the "beloved disciple" and claim that this—otherwise anonymous—disciple's greater authority ensures the truth of his gospel? Could a fisherman from Galilee have written the elegant, spare, philosophically sophisticated prose of this gospel?

—Elaine Pagels, *Beyond Belief,* page 60

The Gospel of John mentions the Beloved Disciple in the context of being the "confidante" of Jesus, a role that Mary Magdalene played. The author also claims that the Beloved Disciple stood at the foot of the cross and comforted Jesus' mother. Mary Magdalene was there. The gospel tells us that Jesus had a mysterious mission for the Beloved Disciple, one that he refused to discuss with Peter, even when Peter asked Jesus probative questions. Was Mary Magdalene the writer, the authority, or the eyewitness source for this gospel? Scholars continue to struggle over this issue, and for now it remains one of the mysteries swirling around Mary Magdalene's life.

Perhaps Mary Magdalene led that first community of Jesus' disciples from the time of Jesus' death until perhaps A.D. 70 or 80. Of course, by the end of this period she would have passed away. But the Jesus community would have had many written and oral stories already in circulation—the initial version of a gospel—that pointed to Mary Magdalene's role as its leader and heroine.

Peter's Story Gains Prominence

The early Christian community seems to have divided its followers along two lines—those who believed that Mary Magdalene should be the head of their church (she certainly seemed to be in the Gnostic view) and those who thought that Peter should wield the absolute power and authority. By A.D. 70, gospels, letters, sermons, and sayings were finally being written. (The Gospel of Mark, believed to be the first gospel, was written in A.D. 70.) All of these writings together made up the earliest beginnings of the New Testament.

In general, however, the rhetoric against women continued. When the Council at Nicaea met in A.D. 325 to decide which texts would be approved for the canon of the Church, the bishops chose the Gospels of Matthew, Mark, Luke, and John. Was it just by chance that those four gospels contained the fewest references to Mary Magdalene, while other texts—in particular the Gnostic gospels—that esteemed her were excluded? Was it coincidence that Peter's version gave him a measure of greater importance? Had it crossed anyone's mind at the Council of Nicaea that subsequent generations of popes might have a problem tracing their apostolic lineage and authority to a woman?

Early Christians would have had to consider that, during those earliest centuries, claiming a woman as spiritual heiress and mother of the Church could bring embarrassment and perhaps even condemnation upon them. Couldn't they get more male converts by being able to point to a founding father rather than a founding mother? There may have been a consensus

Of the hundreds of paintings of Mary Magdalene in the world today, four prominent ones hang in the National Gallery of Art in Washington, D.C.

1. *Madonna and Child with Saint Mary Magdalene and Saint Catherine*, Pietro Lorenzetti, Sienese, c. A.D. 1306 (middle of three panels; tempera on panel and transferred to canvas)

2. *Repentant Magdalen*, Gerard Seghers, Flemish, c. A.D. 1630 (oil on canvas)

3. *The Crucifixion with the Virgin, Saint John, Saint Jerome, and Saint Mary Magdalene*, Pietro Perugino, Umbrian, c. A.D. 1482–1484 (left panel; oil on panel transferred to canvas)

4. *The Magdalen*, Berardino Luini, Milanese, c. A.D. 1525 (oil on panel)

that Mary Magdalene's role needed to be diminished and more credibility and weight given to Peter's.

For a couple of centuries after Jesus' death, the New Testament was being written and possibly revised. Certainly, as it was translated from the oral Aramaic into Greek writing and then into other languages, words and meanings were altered. Aramaic is almost a dead language now and is still spoken only by a handful of people in a village in what is now Syria. The point is that in the translating and transcribing of the Bible, not all words easily translated from one language into another or retained exactly the same meaning. Some say that the Bible may have become more patriarchal in its language through the centuries.

Sadly, the Galilean Aramaic spoken by Jesus may disappear altogether within a generation or two. The version of Aramaic spoken where the Christians settled in the Euphrates Valley was known as Syriac, and it was written with a different script. Religious documents written in Syriac still exist on papyri, and the closest the world can get to original translations is to refer to whatever documents have survived and already been translated.

Mary Magdalene Written Out of the Sacred Narrative

An interesting theory about Mary Magdalene being the author of the fourth gospel is found in an Internet article written by Ramon K. Jusino, M.A., who bases his hypothesis on the research of leading Catholic biblical scholar Raymond E. Brown (*www.BelovedDisciple.org*). In "Mary Magdalene: Author of the Fourth Gospel?" Jusino theorizes that in the history of the early Church there was a fundamental disagreement that brought about a schism, dividing the community into two main groups: the Gnostics and the orthodox believers.

Both groups possessed the fourth gospel. The Gnostic version kept Mary's prominence and identified her as the spiritual leader and heiress of Jesus' sacred teachings. The other group, which favored male apostolic succession, recognized Peter as founding father. At issue for the latter group was the Gospel of John. A revision was needed—not a retouching of the facts or essential elements of known stories about Jesus, but rather an obscuring of Mary Magdalene's identity (perhaps making her instead the Beloved Disciple) and diminishing those portions of the narrative naming her. Accordingly, the result of that rewriting yielded the Gospel of John that appears in the New Testament today.

Medieval Reverence for Mary Magdalene

According to an old legend, the Duke of Burgundy set about building a monastery in Vézelay, France, in the year A.D. 769, and he wanted the relics of Mary Magdalene for the church. He sent one of the monks to Aix (in the south) to fetch Mary Magdalene's remains. The monk found a marble headstone with Mary Magdalene's story chiseled onto it. Waiting until after dark, the monk went to the grave, opened it, and took out the reliquary containing the saint's remains. Under cover of darkness, he took the container back to his lodging. Suddenly, Mary Magdalene appeared and told him not to be afraid and encouraged him to finish what he had set out to do. The next day the monk returned to the monastery. During the last mile to Vézelay, his arms grew weary and he could no longer carry the reliquary. Monks with their abbot leading them miraculously appeared in a procession to carry Mary Magdalene's remains into the new monastery. The legend states that in the monastery of Vézelay, the adoration of Mary Magdalene has resulted in many miracles.

This is just one story that illustrates the way Mary Magdalene's popularity swelled in Europe during the Middle Ages. During that dark period in women's history, Mary Magdalene stood as the patron saint of moral rebirth and regeneration, loving service, active charity, and contemplative withdrawal. Medieval France and England, especially, venerated her. In England, more than 200 ancient churches were established in her name. Both Oxford (where the students were all men) and Cambridge have colleges dedicated to her. Many of the churches and buildings dedicated to Mary Magdalene feature friezes, sculptures, and other types of art depicting her.

Mary Magdalene's Portrayal in Art

The powerful archetypal image of a fallen woman who repented her sins has fueled artists' imagination through the centuries, and some of the greatest painters of all time have produced priceless images of this mythical Mary Magdalene. She has been depicted as the seductive temptress, a full-bosomed woman with bright cheeks, alabaster skin, and long, flowing locks of gold or red. She is shown either on her knees with an unguent jar after the Crucifixion, as seen in Rembrandt's *The Risen Christ Appearing to Mary Magdalene*, or in penitent poses weeping—hence the linkage between Magdalene and the word "maudlin." In religious art, her hair color has special symbolism, and the artists who painted her image undoubtedly knew the meaning of the color they chose. Long hair has been an endur- ing symbol for life force, independence, and an unmarried state. Red hair has been associated with passion, danger, excitement, and energy, whereas golden tresses have represented power.

In Titian's painting, *Penitent Magdalene*, Mary Magdalene's hand rests against her ample bust while her eyes turn upward to Heaven. Rubens portrayed her in his *Christ at Simon the Pharisee* as a kneeling penitent with long, honey-colored hair falling seductively over a bare shoulder and back. She kisses Jesus' leg at the ankle while holding His foot in her hand, His toes close to her partially exposed bosom. Her unguent jar sits nearby. Giotto pained her nude with only her long reddish-gold tresses concealing her vulnerability. Boticelli's work, *Magdalene at the Foot of the Cross*, shows the battle of evil forces to the left of a crucified Jesus. St. Michael slays a serpent on the right, and a repentant Magdalene in a red cloak (symboliz- ing passionate carnality) is prostrate at the base of the cross. In Tintoretto's painting, *Christ in the House of Mary and Martha*, Mary Magdalene's hair is modestly covered, but she appears stunningly draped in a garment made of yards of shimmering blue fabric. Jesus and Mary Magdalene are both draped in this fabric. It is as if the artist were making a point that their "cov- ering" was not different. They had "put on" the same holy cloth of beliefs (the color blue symbolizes the eternal, chaste, and pure).

Perhaps now that Mary Magdalene's story is being revisited and retold in new, more accurate ways, newly interpreted art will follow. Perhaps art- ists will cease to depend upon the tired old archetype of the fallen woman/

repentant sinner and instead depict Mary Magdalene as an important ancestress of the Christian faith, beloved of Jesus, the Thirteenth Apostle, and Woman Who Knows All.

The Modern Church Reverses Itself

It's only taken two millennia, but Mary Magdalene's reputation and role as an important (perhaps preeminent) disciple are being revisited, revised, and repaired. Although the Vatican has reversed its position that Mary was ever a prostitute and revised its missal to reflect that fact, and even though Pope John Paul II proclaimed her the Apostle to the Apostles, many modern people still think of her as the repentant, sinful prostitute. Perhaps because of centuries of patristic Bible interpretations (not to mention the innumerable revisions and translations) or perhaps because of her inaccurate representations in art, Mary Magdalene was written off and written out of the Gospels. Now, in the twenty-first century, that is changing. Efforts of modern scholars, feminists, theologians, historians, writers, and Christians who believe Mary Magdalene has been unfairly treated for far too long are working to give this woman of spirit a higher profile.

Prayer to Saint Mary Magdalene

BLESSED SAINT MARY MAGDALENE, whose beautiful image has been a source of inspiration for artists through the centuries, help us to ever remember the glorious world our awesome God created for us. When we witness a stunning sunset on a summer's eve, silvery moonlight on autumn leaves, spring blooms swaying in a breeze, and glistening snow on winter trees, help us remember the One who created each magnificent scene. Help us to remember God created us in His image, and we are lovely and perfect in His sight. Inspire us to be ever conscious that, within us, we carry the beauty of the Divine. Whether we traverse the road of life buffeted by wild winds of adversity or caressed by breezes of peace, may we know that behind it all is the unseen hand of our Creator. Holy Saint Mary Magdalene, may we be bold and confident and inspired to follow your example of love, inviolable and ever constant—for God and His magnificent Son, our Savior, Lord Jesus. Amen.

Chapter 6

SUPPOSITION, INNUENDO, AND FACTS
FROM OTHER SOURCES

Let him kiss me with the kisses of his mouth:
for thy love is better than wine.
—Song of Solomon 1:2

W hat are we to make of Mary Magdalene's love for Jesus? Was hers the love of a student for her teacher . . . a woman's love for a man . . . or the love of a devoted wife? Upon Jesus' death, did she become the pious widow? Many people think the idea is preposterous, but also puzzling and intriguing. Yet a cadre of Mary Magdalene aficionados will swear that it's more likely than not. Scholars and nonscholars debate the nature of the intimacy between Mary Magdalene and Jesus while the rest of us fuel our water-cooler discussions, coffee-break chatter, and pillow talk with our own speculation. Were they or weren't they married?

Jesus' Pious Widow?

The Church's view is that Mary Magdalene's love for Jesus was that of gratitude, awe, and reverence. After His death, her love became sublime, like that of other female saints and mystics who saw Him as their celestial spouse. While many people believe that Jesus was committed to doing His father's work on Earth and chose the bachelor's life, the Church, in fact, has not forcefully disputed that He might have married. His kissing Mary Magdalene, often on the lips as written in the Gospel of Philip, suggests they shared special feelings.

You can just imagine how significant these kisses were, considering the time in which these two lived. A woman didn't even dare unbind her hair and let it hang while associating with a man who was not her husband, let alone kiss him in public. And yet women and men must have felt attracted to one another. Perhaps some even had the courage to express it. The Song of Solomon, love poems found in the Old Testament and popular in Palestine during Mary Magdalene's lifetime, has long been associated with Mary Magdalene and her love for Jesus, even though the love poem predates them. The Song is an evocative piece with sexual emphasis on a bride's love and yearning for her bridegroom that some say characterizes the Lord as the lover and His people as the beloved. In the following verse, the bride speaks:

> I sleep, but my heart waketh: it is the voice of my beloved that knocketh, saying, Open to me, my sister, my love, my dove, my undefiled: for my head is filled with dew, and my locks with the drops of the night.
>
> I have put off my coat; how shall I put it on? I have washed my feet, how shall I defile them?

—Song of Solomon 5:2–3

Christian writers used the Song as an allegory for the love between Israel and God and also between the Church and Christ. Others have asserted that the Song of Solomon speaks directly to the romantic love the bride (Mary Magdalene) felt for her bridegroom (Jesus). In Genesis, it says that God created us as men and women and gave us sexual communion so that we could experience the same depths of love and commitment for one another that God feels for us. The unmarried apostle Paul said that men should love their wives as their own bodies. Marriage completes the covenant humans have with God to partner and produce children, thus propagating our species.

In fact, Jewish holy men in biblical times were considered incomplete unless they were married. Girls were often pledged to husbands while they were very young. And while many theologians scoff at the idea that Jesus would have married because he would have been considered incomplete if He had not, others agree that He would have been expected to marry, just as He would have been expected to care for His mother after the death of His stepfather Joseph. But if Mary Magdalene was Jesus' widow, why did He not, when He was on the cross, entrust her care to a brother disciple as He did for His mother?

Besides this speculation about marriage, some followers held other views with regard to the relationship between Mary and Jesus.

The Wisdom Chalice

Mary Magdalene as consort and wife to Jesus, according the Gnostic Christian view, magnifies Mary Magdalene and does not diminish Jesus. Mary Magdalene may have been an enlightened woman, privy to all of Jesus' secret teachings. His light would have poured into her and hers into Him in the *hieros gamos*, or sacred marriage. She would have been the wisdom chalice that bore all Jesus' teachings found in the Gospels, and apostolic succession would have flowed from her. It is an interesting idea and one that inspires Mary Magdalene's followers today to feel that she is their spiritual ancestress, teacher, and priestess.

Widow Priestess

If the Gnostic Christians exalted Mary as a high priestess, did she wear robes of purplish-blue heavily embroidered in bright colors, as was typical of women's clothing in her region? Or did she choose the simple white garment of a chaste holy woman or the black garb of a widow (also the color worn by a Nazarite high priestess, according to one account)? In some circles, today, she is revered as a holy priestess. To the Roman Catholic faithful, she is Apostle to the Apostles, and in the Eastern Orthodox Church, Mary Magdalene is called *Isapostolos* (equal to the apostles) and is declared to be the woman who brings glory to all spiritual women, but neither church infers marriage from the close relationship between Mary Magdalene and Jesus. While some readers of *The Da Vinci Code* may be left with the impression that she was both widow and high priestess, many scholars of church history think not.

Mary's Linkage with Israel's Royal Bloodline

One theory purports that Mary Magdalene and Mary of Bethany are the same woman and that she was forced to flee Jerusalem while pregnant with a child whose lineage came from two of Israel's great tribes—the tribe of Benjamin (Mary of Bethany's tribe) and the tribe of Judah (Jesus' tribe).

A child of Jesus, the anointed Son of David of the House of Judah, and Mary of Bethany (a.k.a. Mary Magdalene), the wealthy Benjamite woman, would have merged these two great dynasties. Their child would have carried forth the bloodline of the Holy Grail. If true, then the wife and child would be the hope of the occupied nation of Jews and at the same time a threat to the occupying Romans and those loyal to Herod.

The identity of this royal bloodline, according to *The Da Vinci Code* as well as *Holy Blood, Holy Grail* and *The Woman with the Alabaster Jar*, would have to be hidden because members of Jesus' family would have been singled out for death. Precious few could know about the wife and child of the King of the Jews, and those who did know would have to protect the secret with their lives.

According to various legends, some of which are mentioned in previous chapters, Mary Magdalene gave birth to a daughter, the ancestress to the line of French Merovingian kings, while fleeing the Holy Land for France. Several prominent Europeans today can supposedly trace their bloodlines back to the child of Mary Magdalene and Jesus. You can see how this chain of events could have monumental repercussions for the Church. As mentioned in Chapter 2, the secret society known as the Prieuré de Sion (Priory of Sion) took charge of safeguarding the secret of the Grail and protecting the descendants, along with any proof of the sacred royal bloodline.

The Priory of Sion/Magdalene Connection

The Priory of Sion established the Order of the Knights Templar—those zealous mystical knights whose white mantles boldly sported a red cross.

Some people claim that over time the two organizations virtually became one, although others dispute that assertion. The Templars attracted such notables as Leonardo Da Vinci, Sir Isaac Newton, Botticelli, Victor Hugo, Jean Cocteau, and others, perhaps because they provided members with material and social advancement and embraced ideology more in line with the Gnostics than the Church.

The authors of *Holy Blood, Holy Grail* provide an intriguing list of the Priory of Sion's grand masters, taken from a secret French dossier. Other sources say that in addition to those who presided over the secret society, it attracted many others, including at least one pope. Through the centuries, the Templars acquired tremendous wealth and power. Indeed, the Templars were responsible for building some of the most beautiful Gothic Notre Dame cathedrals in Europe. Some believe the Church felt threatened and sought to eliminate them and seize their wealth, as well as suppress the Templars' secret about the origins of Christianity.

 SECRET FEMININE SYMBOLS IN GOTHIC ARCHITECTURE

While many people might consider the Gothic churches masculine in appearance, experts say many feminine symbols are visible as well. In addition to those listed below, others include spirals, whirls, and columns (especially in crypts or tombs, which also signify the womb). Further study of the Templars will reveal the special meanings that certain symbols held for them.

Arch: The Gothic arch is a symbol of the feminine womb since woman is receptor, carrier, and the one who nourishes life.

Circle: The circle is a symbol of perfection. In the cathedral at Chartres, France, the maze (see the reference to "maze" that follows) is circular, comprising an area of only forty feet.

Lily: France's fleur-de-lis emblem, derived from a stylized lily, is associated with royal power. In the Christian tradition, the lily symbolizes innocence and purity. Many images of saints on holy cards, for example, depict them holding lilies.

Mandorla or seed shape: This ancient symbol represents female divinity and has been found in art engraved on rocks that date to 30,000 B.C.

Maze: The maze has long been a symbol of the process of self-discovery. Moving along a labyrinth or maze, one is said to pass symbolically through initiation, return to the womb, be reborn, and end at one's spiritual center. For some, walking a labyrinth symbolizes a pilgrimage. Many great cathedrals in Europe have mazes or labyrinths.

Rose: This flower was an ancient Roman symbol for sacred prostitutes and was alternately called the Flower of Venus. Sub rosa, meaning something spoken secretly, privately, and confidentially, grew out of the practice of using a rose at meetings where those assembled had to swear to secrecy. If you swore upon the rose, others could be confident that the secret would be kept. The sexual connotation of sub rosa was "under the rose," suggestive of secret sexual mysteries. Troubadours from the south of France adopted the rose as their symbol since their songs were often about love.

Spider webs: These symbolize the manifesting of heavenly or divine gifts. Weaving, whether done by a spider or a woman, is associated with feminine creation.

The Holy Land served as the Templars' initial base. Later they moved their headquarters to Languedoc-Roussillon, a region in southern France where there are many churches dedicated to Mary Magdalene. The Templars venerated Mary Magdalene as the Black Madonna and also associated her with the ancient Egyptian goddess Isis, to whom they also paid homage. The goddess of fertility, Isis was also a Black Madonna. In Aramaic, Jesus' everyday language, black meant "sorrowful," and the expression fit both Mary Magdalene and Isis, who both mourned the loss of their beloveds. (You'll learn more about the Black Madonna in the following section.) In fact, one theory purports that Mary Magdalene may have been a pagan priestess in the Isis cult before meeting Jesus—an idea that orthodox Christians find heretical.

The Templars were devoted to Sophia, Goddess of Wisdom, and saw in Mary Magdalene the embodiment of Sophia. It's confusing to think of Mary Magdalene as the Black Madonna, the embodiment of Sophia, and a priestess of the Isis cult who practiced the ancient rites of anointing and the *hieros gamos*, but the Knights Templar and the Priory of Sion's beliefs suggest all of those associations. For them, Mary Magdalene's anointing of Jesus reenacted an ancient pagan rite. In the anointing, He became the Messiah, a word that comes from the Hebrew word *māshach*, which means "to anoint." The Greek word "Christos" means "anointed one."

Mary Magdalene's anointing prepared Jesus for His participation in the ancient rites of *hieros gamos* and ritual death. Their sacred union, believed to bestow spiritual enlightenment, was not the commonly understood convention of marriage. The lyrics in the Song of Solomon, long associated with Mary Magdalene, are hymns characterized as Tantric, meaning sacredly erotic, even sexual.

> *How fair and how pleasant art thou, O love, for delights!*
> *This thy stature is like to a palm tree, and thy breasts to clusters of grapes.*
> *I said, I will go up to the palm tree; I will take hold of the boughs thereof: now also thy breasts shall be as clusters of the vine, and the smell of thy nose like apples;*
> *And the roof of thy mouth like the best wine for my beloved, that goeth down sweetly, causing the lips of those that are asleep to speak.*
> *I am my beloved's, and his desire is toward me.*
> —SONG OF SOLOMON 7:6–10

According to scholars, the Song text may have been part of an ancient marriage liturgy. In fact, the canonical gospels address Jesus as the "bridegroom." And the Gnostic gospels suggest that Mary Magdalene was His bride. Their union brought *gnosis*, or knowledge. The Gospel of Philip lists five sacraments in order of importance: baptism, anointing, Eucharist, redemption, and bridal chamber. John the Baptist baptized Jesus, but Mary Magdalene anointed him and then supposedly loved Jesus in the bridal chamber, suggesting that her acts exceeded John's in their importance to the Messiah's journey. This emphasis on Mary Magdalene was typically Gnostic.

Mary Magdalene, the Black Madonna, and the Romany

Take a trip to southern France, and it will soon become obvious that Mary Magdalene has a presence there. It is an area of the world uniquely known for its Black Madonnas, or as the French called them, "*Vierge Noires*." Such dark-skinned images of Mother Mary most often take the form of a painting or statue. But are they depicting the Holy Mother of Jesus? In certain places, these Black Madonnas are most often associated with Mary Magdalene, whose cult, some say, had its center in Rennes-le-Chateau, where the Saint Mary Magdalene Church stands. This area of France, as already noted in Chapter 2, was the region of mysteries associated with the Knights Templar. In some instances, the statue of a Black Madonna takes on the color of the material used to create it: for example, different types of marble or wood. Others, such as Our Lady of Rocamadour, have darkened over time from exposure to candle and incense smoke.

According to legends, certain pilgrims have for centuries venerated the Black Madonnas as Mary Magdalene and have left behind gifts and tokens of thanks for miraculous healing and answered prayers. As the legend goes, these Black Madonnas are dark to signify the mysterious truth about Mary Magdalene as the wife of Jesus and bearer of His child. Others say that the Black Madonna represents the hidden feminine qualities of the Greek goddesses Isis, Aphrodite, and Demeter and that these Madonnas hold the keys to transformation. New Age practitioners who study energy fields on Earth will tell you that where the Black Virgins (Madonnas) are located, you will find leylines and energy vortices. According to such practitioners, the Black Madonna, in association with these subtle energy fields around her, awakens the spiritual pilgrim to a higher consciousness. Some even call her the Black Madonna, an Icon for Awakening.

FAST FACTS : France's Black Madonnas

The beautiful Dark or Black Madonnas are found in many places in the world today, including Spain, Germany, Sicily, Mexico, Costa Rica, France, and even the United States (in Missouri). They pay homage to the Blessed Virgin and are often called the Black Virgins. However, in southern France, as noted in the main text of this section, they are frequently associated with Mary Magdalene. Some of the most notable Black Madonnas include the following:

Black Madonna of Le Puy, located in Notre Dame de France, in Le Puy-en-Valey

Black Madonna of the Cathedral de Notre Dame, located in Paris's Notre Dame cathedral

Black Madonna of Marceille (sic), located in Limoux near Rennes-le-Chateau

Black Madonna of Rocamadour, located in the chapel of Saint Saviour's Church in Rocamadour

Notre Dame Sous Terre (Our Lady under the Earth), located in the crypt of Notre Dame de Chartres in Chartres, south of Paris

Saint Sara-la-Kâli, Patron Saint of the Gypsies, located in the Notre Dame de la Mer Church in the town of Les Saintes Maries de la Mer

The patron saint of the Romany (Gypsies) is Sara-la-Kâli (Sara the Black and also Sarah the Gitane), who some claim is also a Black Madonna. Each year the Romany travel from all over the world to descend on Les Saintes Maries de la Mer (the Saints Marys of the Sea) to pay respect to Saint Sarah. The Romany believe that Sarah was a Gypsy who lived near the seashore and rescued Mary Magdalene and her traveling companions from their oarless boat. The Romany's destination is the village chapel dedicated to the Marys. Lighting candles, they recite prayers and invocations and present their children to the statue of Sarah.

One legend describes Sarah as the Egyptian servant of Mary Jacobi. Yet another legend says that Martha, Lazarus, Maximinus, Cedonius (the blind man), Sarah the servant girl, and others were in the oarless boat with Mary Magdalene. According to this legend, the group built an oratory that was eventually replaced by a fortified church, Notre Dame de la Mer (Our Lady of the Sea).

The Tarot's Female Pope

The French Romany didn't create the Tarot deck of cards, but they did use them for divination. Even today, if you visit the Les Saintes Maries de la Mer during May when they make their annual pilgrimage, you may find some willing to tell your fortune. The Tower, one of seventy-eight cards in the deck, was associated with Mary Magdalene because of her origins in Magdala. As mentioned in Chapter 1, the Aramaic name for Magdala is Migdal Nunya (Tower of Fish).

In addition to the Tower, in medieval Tarot cards the female pope card was also associated with Mary Magdalene. An old legend details how a woman disguised as a male was admitted to the priesthood and rose through ecclesiastical ranks to become pope. She was referred to as Papesse Jeanne, who represented the church that venerated Mary Magdalene as its matriarch. Author Margaret Starbird gives a detailed account of this Tarot card and others in *The Woman with the Alabaster Jar, Mary Magdalene and the Holy Grail*.

Mary Magdalene also graces a Renaissance Tarot card as she stands vigil at the entry to Christ's empty tomb. She is the gatekeeper, guardian of sacred truth, hidden secrets, as yet unrevealed knowledge, and mystery. Her image symbolizes knowledge gained through mystical experience and intuition, another instance in which she is associated with hidden knowledge.

The Second Eve

Have you ever thought about how the stories of Mary Magdalene and Eve might be linked? Feminists see it immediately. Here's a quick review of Eve's story: God created Adam and put him in the Garden of Eden. He warned Adam not to eat from the Tree of the Knowledge of Good and Evil. Then God made Adam sleep. Thinking that Adam might be lonely, God fashioned a woman from Adam's rib, and Adam named her Eve. Satan, in the form of a serpent, tempted Eve to eat fruit from the forbidden tree. Perhaps hungry for knowledge and desiring to be wise, Eve ate that particular fruit.

And the serpent said unto the woman, Ye shall not surely die: For God doth know that in the day ye eat thereof, then your eyes shall be opened, and ye shall be as gods, knowing good and evil.

—Genesis 3:4–5

In her generosity, Eve also offered some to Adam. When God questioned Adam about how he suddenly knew he was naked, Adam blamed Eve.

And the man said, The woman whom thou gavest to be with me, she gave me of the tree, and I did eat.

—Genesis 3:12

As for Eve, she answered God truthfully when He asked her what she had done.

. . . And the woman said, The serpent beguiled me, and I did eat.

—Genesis 3:13

Their act of defiance became known as the original sin. It meant that they would no longer see with God's eyes of perfection, but would see imperfectly from then on. There are many different viewpoints of how that sin has affected the morality of Adam and Eve's descendants—all of us.

Here's the linkage: Eve was tempted by Satan and banished from the Garden of Eden by God the Father. Mary Magdalene suffered from mental illness until she was healed by Jesus, the Son of God. Both women hungered for knowledge. Eve got hers from the forbidden fruit. Mary

Magdalene received hers from Jesus. He praised her for wanting to know more about God.

> . . . *Mary hath chosen that good part; which shall not be taken away from her.*

> —LUKE 10:42

According to Genesis, God listed three ways He would punish Eve: He would greatly multiply her sorrow in conception, cause her to bring forth children in sorrow, and have her desire her husband only to be ruled by him. As for Mary Magdalene, her punishment for knowledge came when the disciples told her they didn't believe she could have seen Jesus in a vision. They also denied that she could have received a secret teaching from Jesus. They even doubted her story about the Resurrection and ran to the tomb to see for themselves. Eve was punished immediately with banishment from the garden, while Mary Magdalene suffered an immediate reactionary rebuke from the disciples, who thought she'd concocted a story about receiving a vision of Jesus and a secret teaching. Then, Pope Gregory I branded her a prostitute, a falsehood perpetuated by the clergy for nearly two millennia. It is also interesting that although both women played important roles, they are rarely mentioned in the Scriptures. Eve is mentioned twice in the Old Testament and Mary Magdalene's name appears no more than fourteen times in the canonical gospels.

MYSTICAL CONNECTIONS

Some writers see a mystical, symbolic connection between Eve and Mary Magdalene. In the creation story from the book of Genesis, the female was taken from Adam's side. (Some say God improved upon His "first draft" and created woman.) Eve, by "knowing" Adam in intimate sexual union, became his wife. Traditionally, many Judeo-Christian men think that God made women inferior and subordinate to men. But God, through Jesus, showed the world a different way to view and treat women. From her time until now, Mary Magdalene, the woman closest to Jesus, has epitomized the intellectual prowess, spiritual acumen, and personal power that women not only possess but often use for good in the world.

In Jesus' case, when He was crucified, His side was pierced, and water and blood flowed out. Just as water could be symbolic of baptism and the blood could represent wine (the new covenant), the flowing out could be symbolic of his mystical wife—the Church—coming into being. In that sense, Mary Magdalene and all men and women who together made up the Church became Jesus' wife/bride through His death and resurrection.

Pagan Goddess and the Gospel

Earlier in this chapter, the connection between Mary Magdalene and the pagan goddess Isis was briefly noted, but there's more to it than just the Black Madonna connection. In some ways, Mary Magdalene's role in the Easter story also parallels the pagan goddess Isis and her god/consort/husband Osiris. Like Jesus, Osiris was put to death on a Friday. Both

Mary Magdalene and Isis mourned the loss of their beloveds. Isis traveled far and wide searching for the body of Osiris, who had been dismembered. Because of Isis' love (and magic), after three days Osiris arose from the dead. The authors of *The Templar Revelations* reveal that both Isis and Mary Magdalene, while searching for their respective loved ones' bodies, made statements eerily similar about not knowing where the body had been taken. Also, the authors point out that while Isis went into Hades (often depicted as a cave) to retrieve her risen lord, Mary Magdalene went to the sepulcher. Some people point to these similarities and suggest that Mary Magdalene and Jesus were reenacting the Egyptian Osiris' resurrection story.

Another highly controversial theory is that Mary Magdalene was formerly a sacred temple worker in the Temple of Isis. Temple workers healed or helped others transcend the material world in order to reach spiritual realms, and they used their bodies to do it. They were not prostitutes in the context of how we think of such women today; rather, they were powerful priestesses who could enable others to experience a higher form of spirituality through sacred sex. In the temples, they represented the temple's patron goddess.

There have been similar examples of such women in history: the Greek *heterae* (women who served as sacred paramours and concubines) and the Indian *Shaktas* (women who worshipped Shakti, the feminine creative part of God). These women were knowledgeable about Tantric sex as a means of achieving a higher state of consciousness.

The sexual union has been a natural impulse in men and women since Adam and Eve. In fact, the word "union," mentioned in the first book of

Ways to Invoke the Holy Blessings of Saint Mary Magdalene

Make a batch of *navette*. These cylindrical French pastries are shaped like a boat to commemorate the arrival of Mary Magdalene, Mary of Bethany, Martha, Lazarus, and Sarah in Les Saintes Maries de la Mer. It is traditional to make and offer these pastries on February 2 to mark the arrival of the saints and also to serve them for the *Féte de la Chandeleur*, or Candlemas procession. (Candlemas is the feast day celebrating Jesus' first presentation in the Temple following His birth.) Find the recipe for *Navette à la Fleur d'Oranger* at *www.beyond.fr/food/navette.html*, or make the traditional version of *Navettes de la Chandeleur* found in Provence: *www.frenchfood.about.com/library/blnavettes.htm*.

Plant a rose garden in the spring. Fill it with the Mary Magdalene rose, introduced by English rose breeder David Austin. The pink/apricot bloom's scent is a blend of myrrh and tea rose. Let your rose garden be a living symbol of the mystery of divine love. Remember that during the Middle Ages, Mary Magdalene was referred to as Mystic Rose and simply The Rose. The white rose traditionally has been an emblem of the Blessed Virgin Mary because it symbolizes purity and virginity. The red or pink rose stands for passion, desire, beauty, and perfection—symbols for Saint Mary Magdalene.

Paint a maze or labyrinth. You might do this on a canvas floor cloth or on your deck. Or create one in your garden using pebbles for paths that are broken by ground cover or grass.

Visit the Russian Church of Mary Magdalene on the Mount of Olives. Located on the east side of Jerusalem, it was built in 1886 by Tsar Alexander the Third. This beautiful church features traditional Russian architecture with its feminine onion-shaped domes. It is dedicated to Miriam from Migdal (Mary Magdalene).

Affirmations

- *I open my heart, asking God to magnify my love for the Lord and His saints, especially Saint Mary Magdalene.*

- *I will visit the Garden of Eden within and walk with my Creator to better understand the temptations of life and how to spiritually deal with them.*

the Bible, meant "knowing," and another word for *knowing* is the Gnostic term *gnosis*.

And Adam knew Eve his wife; and she conceived . . . .

—GENESIS 4:1

In the history of the Bible, sex has always been one of those topics sure to stir controversy. The Old Testament tells how, in some cases, men who couldn't conceive with their wives took concubines to produce an heir. And yet, one of the Ten Commandments clearly states that people should not commit adultery.

Although the apostle Paul knew that many of the apostles, being traditional Jewish men, were married, he also expressed his support of the unmarried, celibate priestly state. He recognized that being unmarried freed a minister of the faith from familial duties and worldly concerns. If men who came to the Christian way unmarried remained celibate, he reasoned, they could focus more on the work of the Church.

The official mandate for celibacy came at the behest of Pope Siricius, who abandoned his wife and children in order to secure the position of pope. He then declared no priest could sleep with his spouse. In fact, prior to his declaration, two different meetings or councils of the early Church

Affirmations

❧ *I offer myself as a vessel, like Saint Mary Magdalene did, to anoint others with healing love. I will silently bless each person I meet this day with the words, "I give you my love."*

(the Spanish Council of Elvira in the second century and the First Council of Aries in A.D. 314) legislated rules forbidding all priests, deacons, and bishops to engage in conjugal relations with their wives. To breach the rules meant exclusion from the clergy. Pope Siricius, in A.D. 385, issued the papal decree enforcing the rules, and Pope Gregory VII in 1139 definitively set forth the Church's decree for all time that the priesthood would be comprised only of unmarried, celibate men. The Church's position is that it is simply continuing a tradition dating back to the earliest Church fathers, even the apostles.

Prayer to Saint Mary Magdalene

BLESSED MARY MAGDALENE, holy vessel of the Divine spirit of light and love, I consecrate to you my mind, heart, and will. Help me to be a faithful disciple of Jesus. May my devotion to Him be magnified through your grace. Inspire me to be ever mindful of the presence of the Lord and to increase my reverence for Him. May my heart be purified, my sins forgiven, and my understanding of His teachings grow ever more insightful. Holy Mary Magdalene, come to me when my heart feels spiritually dry and infuse me with holy waters of hope. Inspire me to dive ever deeper into the sea of love for God. Bless me with the grace to keep His commandments. Grant me an increase in humility, piety, knowledge, and fortitude. Dearest Saint Mary Magdalene, I invoke you to help me overcome temptation and evil inclinations. Blessed myrrh bearer and light bearer, illuminate my path and guide my steps toward the Divine. Amen.

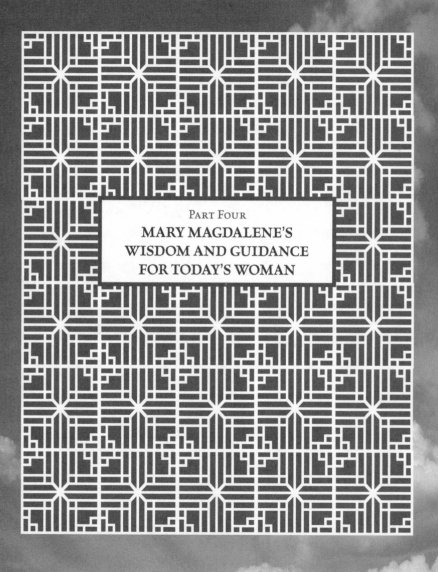

PART FOUR

**MARY MAGDALENE'S
WISDOM AND GUIDANCE
FOR TODAY'S WOMAN**

CHAPTER 7

HOW TO NURTURE YOUR SPIRITUAL SELF

I was sent forth from [the] power,
and I have come to those who reflect upon me,
and I have been found among those who seek after me.
Look upon me, you who reflect upon me,
and you hearers, hear me.
You who are waiting for me, take me to yourselves.
And do not banish me from your sight.
And do not make your voice hate me, nor your hearing.
Do not be ignorant of me anywhere or any time. Be on your guard!
Do not be ignorant of me.
—THE THUNDER: PERFECT MIND VI: 13,
THE NAG HAMMADI LIBRARY

The voice in the above poem is decidedly female. Her name is Thunder. She speaks of that holy power that lies beyond the mind's grasp and extends into the world. She calls us to reflect on and to receive this holy power. We may tell ourselves that we'd love to respond, only later. If you are like most busy people, your days are often overscheduled with activities and flooded with to-do lists. There may be little or no downtime for quiet reflection and the remembrance of sacred things. But to bring more spirituality into your life, you need only to set forth your sacred intention, make your appointment with the Divine the most important part of your day, be courageous about entering into the unknown, and open yourself to receiving whatever gifts may be given to you.

The greatest of all gifts is love. Love is an energy that, unless we impede it, flows outward as reverence toward the Creator and affection toward others. But we must also allow love to flow inward, to us. Jesus made love the centerpiece of His mission on Earth. Mary Magdalene personified that love. We don't have to stop what we are doing in our busy lives to love; we only have to be aware of how we are doing each thing, because love can infuse everything we do.

Mary Magdalene didn't spring from her mother's womb an ecstatic, contemplative saint, filled with light and love. Like all of us, she was imperfect. However, when she met and was healed by Jesus, Mary Magdalene chose to open her life to God's goodness. By being courageous enough to quiet our minds and go deep inside ourselves, all the way down to our core—the taproot of our being—we, like the contemplative Mary Magdalene, will find our own sacred center. It is there we can go for our deepest devotions, our heartfelt prayers of praise and supplication. There, in peace, love, and light, we may ask God for the gifts He desires to give us. And, through our willingness to receive them, we can become inspired and empowered to make good choices for our lives.

. . . Know ye not that your body is the temple of the Holy Ghost which is in you, which ye have of God, and ye are not your own?

—1 Corinthians 6:19

Create Holy Space

Many early Christians prayed in nature—at the seashore, in caves, on hillsides, and in gardens—as well as in the homes of fellow believers and friends. Later, when Christianity became more established, believers practiced their faith in churches but did not abandon home prayer, which sometimes took place in a room with an altar. Any place can be a holy space. Holy space is made so by intention, presence, and prayers. Of course, the holiest space is the temple of your own heart. But most of us desire a physical place too, where we can sit and be still in preparation for entering the temple of our heart.

Spiritual energy, some believe, stays in that physical space where you come again and again to pray, meditate, and contemplate. There are some places in the world, such as sacred sites in the Holy Land and in other countries, where modern-day pilgrims have felt a strong holy "vibration" that they attribute to people having worshipped in that place for centuries, thus spiritualizing it. And while churches, which allow for the gathering together of many, may hold this spiritual energy, Jesus also said he would be present where as few as two or more were gathered in His name. It isn't always possible to get to a church for daily worship, but you do have other options.

Interior Space

Choose a closet, a quiet corner in your house or apartment, a protected space in a garden—all can become your designated holy space. Make the area beautiful. If you're working with indoor space, choose a spot that is quiet, free from foot traffic, and away from telephones, radios, and televisions. Move in a cushion or a chair and a table. Cover the table with a blue, purple, or rose-colored altar cloth (colors associated with Mary Magdalene) and add fresh flowers, incense, candles, rosaries, holy cards, anointing oil, and prayer books. In short, include those things that call you to worship. For added privacy, hide the space using a two- or three-paneled screen. You should feel safe, able to close your eyes and drift deeply into a peaceful state where your mind is no longer filled with the troubles of the world.

And be not conformed to this world: but be ye transformed by the renewing of your mind, that ye may prove what is that good, and acceptable, and perfect, will of God.

—ROMANS 12:2

Garden Space

Create a sanctuary in your own yard or garden by arranging comfortable furniture with cushions, works of yard art, statuary, and aquatic accoutrements (like a fountain or koi pond). Sow some herbs and scented flowers and put in a tree or two (they can be dwarf-sized or in containers if your space is limited). Add some beautiful pique assiette or broken-plate mosaic stepping-stones with spiritual words like *love, blessings, peace, harmony, dreams, wholeness,* and *radiance* placed around the garden. (These words can even be in other languages, if you like.) Hang a wind chime and a birdfeeder. Choose a place in this garden where you will sit to contemplate, pray, and meditate.

Make entering your holy space, whether indoors or outside, the most important part of your daily regimen. Keep your appointment with the sacred source of your being.

I circle around God, around the primordial tower. I've been circling for a thousand years and I still don't know: am I a falcon, a storm, or a great song?
—RANIER MARIA RILKE, *BOOK OF HOURS: LOVE POEMS TO GOD*

"Ich lebe mein Leben.../I live my life in widening", from *Rilke's Book of Hours: Love Poems to God* by Ranier Maria Rilke, translated by Anita Barrows and Joanna Macy, copyright ©1996 by Anita Barrows and Joanna Macy. Used by permission of Riverhead Books, an imprint of Penguin Putnam Inc.

Mary Magdalene entered the temple of her heart and received the gift of a vision of Jesus and a secret teaching, according to the Gospel of Philip. Praying, meditating, and contemplating in sacred space brings peace, energizes the body, reduces stress, and allows for an inflow (or bubbling up) of spiritual knowledge. In that state of mind, we become co-creators with God to manifest what we need and want in our lives.

But seek ye first the kingdom of God, and his righteousness; and all these things shall be added unto you.

—MATTHEW 6:33

Seek Knowledge from a Sacred Source

For Christian mystics and holy people of other great religious traditions, knowledge of self and God become inseparable. In reverential stillness, sacred knowledge comes. Tradition has it that Mary Magdalene spent years in the La Sainte-Baume cave in France in deep contemplation and, probably, spiritual ecstasy.

Other female role models have also set such examples when it comes to seeking spiritual awareness and enlightenment. Hildegard of Bengin, a German medieval mystic and abbess, lived as a recluse in the care of a nun before becoming prioress of a religious community. From her ecstatic visions and revelations, she created sacred art and music, including many new hymns, canticles, and anthems for which she wrote both the music and lyrics. Catherine of Siena, an Italian medieval mystic, was in the middle of prayers when Jesus, His mother, and other heavenly beings paid her visit. Mother Mary took Catherine's hand and held it up to Jesus. He placed a band of gold upon it that was visible forever after to Catherine, but not to others. She wrote a beautiful account of the soul's love for God, which she dictated to a scribe when she was in ecstatic trances.

Wherefore, the eye of the intellect is lifted up and gazes into My Deity, when the affection behind the intellect is nourished and united with me; this is a sight which I grant to the soul, infused with grace, who, in truth, loves and serves Me.

—THE DIALOGUE OF SAINT CATHERINE OF SIENA

Cast Out Your Demons

Mary Magdalene was content to sit with Jesus and listen. As his closest friend and confidante, she must have listened wholly focused on what He was saying, totally present in each moment. Wealth and the material world no longer appealed to her. Her past was dead. Her new life was uncertain. She needed to be fully present in each moment with Jesus. Maybe Mary Magdalene heard what the shamans call the "song," which once perceived is so seductive there is no turning back. Mary Magdalene was now on her spiritual path, and she was listening and receiving in the same way that we listen and receive in contemplation and meditation.

We seem to have lost that connection to the unseen, to the intuitive parts of our nature, the hidden meanings in symbols and signs. Perhaps it's because historically women have been persecuted for their faith. This was especially true during the first centuries and later in the medieval period when women were burned as witches because their spiritual gifts were misunderstood. Modern women have more options for creating spirit-filled lives than our ancient sisters did for expressing theirs. Despite the glass ceilings of the corporate world and the stained-glass ceilings in the ecclesiastical one, women are making great strides and achieving remarkable accomplishments in arenas that once belonged exclusively to men. This competitive drive to do rather than to be, according to some psychologists, is a woman's way of expressing her masculine side in the world.

But a woman's greatest power may lie in her feminine qualities, gifts of spirit, and attributes. The earliest Paleolithic art depicts female nudes who are not engaged in anything. They are simply standing. The late mythologist Joseph Campbell said that their power was in their being, their body, and their presence. He also noted that we mustn't concern ourselves too much with what has happened in history, but with what is happening to us now.

There are many women who are bitterly disappointed at the unfairness of life. Their choices have put them in shackles. In many ways, women can be their own worst enemies. Imagine arriving at the realization that there was a life waiting for you—one that nurtured you and nourished your spirit—but you never lived it. Facing something like that is akin to experiencing that dark night of the soul about which the Christian mystic and poet Saint John of the Cross wrote. What keeps you from following your passion? Perhaps what blocks you are the personal demons of insecurity, low self-esteem, addiction, fear, negative thinking, lack of personal power, feelings of unworthiness, or your own judgmental tendencies as well as the judgments of others. Here are six ways to begin to unblock, reverse course, and point your life in a new direction.

Establish Clear Intentions

Identify the negatives (demons) in your life. Affirm that you want to release them, and begin taking the necessary steps. Don't get disheartened if you find this first step difficult. Old patterns are hard to break. But don't give up. You are not alone. Do you remember Michelangelo's painting on the Sistine Chapel, with God's and Adam's fingers reaching toward one another? When you reach one hand toward God to be lifted up, two great hands come twice as far to meet yours. Envision being freed from every snare and fetter that traps and holds you back from living a rich spiritual life full of passion and love. Remember that your own mind and heart determine your success or failure.

Begin a Process of Self-Discovery and Empowerment

Once you figure out what's not working in your life, choose new spiritual habits that better serve the life you desire. Replace negatives with positives. Don't try to do everything at once. Take your time to eradicate one bad habit and cultivate a new one before moving on to the next. For example, give up mentally and verbally criticizing others and instead try to see people as if through the eyes of Jesus or Mary Magdalene and other saints.

Seek Professional Assistance

Whether it be from a mental health professional, a spiritual counselor, or a physician, seek help if you feel you can't do it alone. There is no shame in asking for help. Remember that God helps those who help themselves. This step can be important if you have deep-seated emotional issues or conflicts. Many issues have to be worked on from the inside, for they may be rooted deep in your psyche and have their basis in childhood or parental pain and disappointment. You may feel stuck in a quagmire of depression, bitterness, or anger. In prayer and meditation, ask the Lord to help you with these problems by giving you the strength to forgive all parties involved and to release the emotion that holds you prisoner. Pray for the courage to seek professional help and the strength to allow the process of healing to begin.

Draw on the Power of Forgiveness

Forgiveness may be one of the greatest gifts you have to bring to healing and wholeness. Accumulated emotional baggage makes an awfully heavy load to carry around. No one escapes hurt and disappointment in life. And some things are so horrendous, you may wonder how the heart could ever let them go and actually forgive the doers of those deeds. You may even feel the fight-or-flight response while simply remembering old arguments or violent encounters. Yet there are many tools in a therapist's bag, including hypnosis, talk therapy, eye movement desensitization response (EMDR), and other techniques that can be of help to you. Forgiving others will free up energy in your body, and then you can channel that energy into constructive spiritual work. Soon, you will begin to feel light on your feet and light on the planet. Joy will replace pain, and bad memories will begin to fade like an old newspaper clipping.

Build a Strong Support Network

Your network could be a few close friends, family members, or other women who share their faith together. Mary Magdalene journeyed with Jesus, but she was also in the company of women. Those women supported one another in their spiritual quest and devotion to Jesus. In addition to solitary work, there is always work to be done in a group.

Spend Time in Prayer Each Day

Make a conscious effort to hold true to this priority. As important as it is to actively praise and petition the Lord, it is equally important to be receptive to the divine guidance that comes.

Develop Good Spiritual Habits

Learn to appreciate and enjoy holy silence. You may have lofty thoughts from time to time, but what is the sum total of every little fleeting thought that runs through your mind every second of the day? Are these thoughts spiritual, positive, and powerful? Someone once said that you must be ever vigilant at the door of your consciousness. Do not let wrong thinking lead you in wrong directions. Unrestrained emotions deplete your stores of energy. Sure, an angry outburst pumps adrenaline into your system while an argument continues. Afterward, however, you feel drained. Emotional confrontation is so depleting that it behooves all of us to find other, more constructive ways to resolve conflict and crisis.

This is not to suggest that passivity is the right way to deal with conflict. It's just far better to discuss the point of contention in a constructive context. Open and frank discussions often lead to positive solutions. Confronting emotional issues in the right way can be cathartic and lead to resolution, which, in turn, restores a state of calmness, even serenity.

Many doctors and health researchers now believe there is a strong mind/body connection at work in our lives. That connection underscores the importance of caring for your physical body so that, when conflicts and emotional issues arise, you have the stamina to deal with them without feeling depleted.

Care for Your Body

Most of us are slaves to our senses. We often don't think about how the food and drink we consume helps or hurts our bodies and brains. Learn to eat sensibly—that includes a balanced diet and six to eight glasses of water throughout the day. Start including some "brain foods" in your diet. Blueberries, salmon, and nuts are just a few that have been shown to benefit the brain. Find an exercise regimen that you like and will stick with, such as walking or yoga.

If your doctor has no objections, set aside some time during the week or the month to fast. A fast doesn't necessarily mean giving up all food and drink for a period of time. It could entail eliminating one food for one day, or it could be having only fruit juice in the morning of a half-day fast. There are many ways to fast. Fasting not only gives your stomach a periodic rest, but when it's combined with affirmation, prayer, and meditation, it also increases your spiritual magnetism or soul power.

Get Enough Sleep

Doctors and scientists stress that sleep is extremely important. Sleep deprivation can lead to a variety of physical, emotional, and mental strains. The demands of our lives often cause us to shortchange our bodies of much-needed sleep. The body, we are told, repairs and heals itself in sleep.

Spiritually speaking, sleep is important for other reasons. Those who keep dream journals know that in sleep, dreams can help solve problems, yield insights into the stresses of life, throw up spiritual messages, and prompt the dreamer to work out relationship conundrums. Medical intuitive Caroline Myss believes that we can work on issues of forgiveness during dream time. When men and women can no longer speak civilly about their relationship problems, one or both can meditate before going to sleep and ask through prayer that the other person meet them in the dream time to work on their situation.

Take Time-Outs to Reclaim Your Connection to God

When you are going about your life at breakneck speed, you probably aren't thinking a whole lot about being centered in peace and calm. But we have to find a balance between our work and family obligations and our alone time. Consider these time-outs as spiritual appointments. Use them to release stress and turn within.

Writer Madeleine L'Engle, in *Walking on Water, Reflections on Faith and Art*, asserted that we must be willing to know things at their deepest, most mythic sense. Instead of fantasizing about the future or remembering the past, we could be fully present in each moment. Collectively, these moments constitute our lives. In meditation, you experience intense awareness although your body is still. In deep stillness, you forget the demands of the senses and make an inner connection with God. This surely must have been Mary Magdalene's experience, because saints and mystics of all religions know this place and go there often to be blessed by the presence of the Divine. You can know it, too. Take the time to dive deeply within. Remember, Jesus said that where your mind is, there you'll find your treasure.

FAST FACTS : Types of Spiritual Retreats

There are many types of retreats available. Some are geared toward specific groups of people, while others focus on various themes. Here are a few examples:

Couples retreat: This type of retreat usually focuses on strengthening love and understanding between married couples and exploring the needs arising from relationship and communication issues.

Guided weekend retreats with a presenter or leader: Getting away from Friday until Sunday can feel like a vacation. This type of retreat is built around a leader or presenter who addresses a specific theme or particular focus.

Teen retreat: Often sponsored by Catholic and Christian schools, this type of retreat addresses youth issues. Speakers challenge as well as affirm teens in discussions about moral and ethical behavior choices and religious teachings.

Women's retreat: Women support other women in their spiritual renewal and practices. The retreat may include sessions of prayer, writing, singing, discussion, lectures, and nature walks.

Men's retreat: Similar to a women's retreat, this type of renewal focuses on issues in men's lives and how to live in a more spiritually balanced way.

Personal empowerment retreat: Whether the focus is on aging, gender issues, grief counseling, or any other issue important to men and women, this type of retreat can be beneficial and rewarding. Such a retreat can take place over a weekend or last a week or more.

Pilgrimage: The journey to a particular spiritual or religious destination is the focus of this type of retreat.

CULTIVATING A SPIRITUAL LIFE

Here are some definitive steps you can take to grow as a more spiritual individual:

Engage in right thinking. Make decisions empowered by your spiritual conviction. Regardless of the spiritual path you choose, support it with right thinking and right action according to the tenets of your faith.

Strive for balanced living. Find a complementary mix of work and leisure, of outer and inner activity, of wakefulness and sleep, of eating and fasting.

Choose friends carefully. A friend is more precious than gold. Surround yourself with friends who support your effort toward claiming a more spiritual life. Don't mix too much with people who easily judge others and are filled with the kind of negative thinking and behavioral tendencies that are counterproductive to a spiritual life.

Practice true humility. Work at lessening the ego's grip over your life. In a "me first" world, humility seems to have fallen away from us. Guests on television and radio talk shows bombard us with messages that practically scream, "It's all about me." They call it promotion. But you can promote something, even be wealthy and famous, without being egotistical. Humility is such a refreshing and beautiful quality; it's well worth cultivating.

Engage in charitable acts that help others less fortunate. Be as generous as you can afford to be with your time and money. Donate to worthwhile causes such as women's shelters and organizations that provide food for homeless families. Purchase medicines or pay for heating and electricity for elderly shut-ins. Remember how Mary Magdalene and her spiritual sisters took care of Jesus and His followers out of their resources, and use that as your example.

Ways to Invoke the Holy Blessings of Saint Mary Magdalene

Create a "Holy Tears" bottle. Find a pretty bottle, preferably blue (for holiness). Adorn it with beads and wire (purchased at craft stores). Place it somewhere in your home where it will remind you of Mary Magdalene's tears of love and sadness during the Passion of Jesus, as well as the Eastern Church's ancient practice of capturing tears shed for a holy purpose.

Sanctify a prayer room. Scent it with oils made from frankincense or myrrh, which are both resins, or use a rose or rose geranium oil. Place the scented oil in a perfume-burning lamp—a china and glass pot or small container with a wick that gets lit and then snuffed out. Let the scent waft through the room, calling you to worship.

Purchase some chanting or devotional music. Listen to this sacred music, commonly referred to as another form of prayer, as you go about your tasks during the day. When you remember God as you listen to devotional music, the work is made holy.

Engage in *lectio divina*. This means celebrating the written and spoken word of God. If you find prayer daunting, try moving into prayer as a response to reading the Scriptures and letting the word of God "speak" directly to you. This practice allows you to experience an exchange between you and your Beloved in much the same way that holy words pregnant with meaning flowed between Mary Magdalene and Jesus.

Affirmations

- *Following Mary Magdalene's example, I am cultivating a personal relationship with Jesus and sharing the love He expresses through me to others.*

- *I listen to the Holy Spirit intoning sacred music inside me, guiding me toward healing and wholeness.*

Another way to nurture your spiritual self is to venture into nature. Perhaps there is a park, garden, lake, or field near where you live or work. Could you retreat there during a lunch break or before or after a long workday? Nature connects us with the innermost parts of ourselves in a deep (some might say mythical) way. We are often energized by nature, even when the weather is uncertain, mirroring our lives. Consider how the sun lights the underside of a thunderhead with the promise of hope, how the sun's rays warm our bodies and lift our spirits, or even how the water reflects a billowy cloud pattern and allows us to feel a harmony we don't find in our homes and offices.

Nature offers us myriad faces, but never the expression of despair. Mary Magdalene and Jesus spent many days with nature around the Sea of Galilee. Though their world was different from ours, it was also the same. Our Earth and sun were also theirs. The stars in our sky are the same stars that were in their sky. The sun still rises and sets; the moon still moves through its phases. As we allow nature to work its magic on us, we can allow thoughts of Jesus and Mary Magdalene to lead us more deeply into a contemplation of the Divine hand behind it all.

Affirmations

❧ On each [name the day of the week], I will go to church for an hour of Eucharistic adoration.

Go on a Spiritual Retreat

References to the word "spirit" are found in many parts of the world. For example, it is translated as *ruah* in Hebrew, *pneuma* in Greek, and *spiritus* in Latin. Our spirit animates our conscious life. It also mediates between our body and mind. When we engage in spiritual practices such as prayer, we are directing our breath, energy, mind, and life force toward God. At the very heart of spirituality is love. The contemplative Mary Magdalene would have understood this. Undoubtedly she would have lived her life expressing her spirituality in the three ways of all spiritual pilgrims: through love and understanding, through good works, and through passionate prayer and devotion.

The reasons for taking a spiritual retreat are varied and highly personal. For some, a retreat is a chance to escape the rat race for a while and recharge depleted batteries. For others, a retreat allows them to move closer to God. A dry heart—one that no longer feels the passionate desire and drive to pursue spiritual practices—can compel a person to seek out a retreat. Still others find that retreating from the day to day draws them deeper into their faith or gives them the opportunity to work on themselves as spiritual beings.

Churches all over the world offer retreats and pilgrimages for weary souls. To find lists of retreats, go to Google and type "retreats" into the search line. To locate retreats focused on Mary Magdalene, type "Mary Magdalene + retreats" instead. You can also visit *www.stmarymagdalene.org* or *www.retreatfinder.com*.

Novena Prayer to Saint Mary Magdalene

SAINT MARY MAGDALENE, come into my heart. I beseech you to hear my prayer of love for myself and for others who desire a spiritual life. We have lost our way, Holy Mother Mary Magdalene. Enable us to hear that inner song. Give us courage to follow our heart, the power to overcome the obstacles in our lives, the passion to pursue our dreams. Help us to manifest those things eluding us that bring joy and peace and understanding and love. Direct our paths to those spiritual beings on earth who will befriend and assist us as we journey toward the Divine. Give us comfort if we do not find the right mate in life right away. Strengthen our resolve. We find hope and take refuge in you who found your greatest love on earth—Jesus. Holy apostle, Mary Magdalene, help us find our way to our own spiritual path and embolden us to put our feet upon it. As in a labyrinth or a maze where the destination is both known and not known, guide our footsteps to the center. Glorious Lady, grant us through your intercession the graces we need for body, mind, and spirit. Especially during this novena, we ask (state your request). Through you may our faith deepen and our love for God be magnified. Amen.

To use this prayer as novena, recite it nine times
in a row for nine days in a row.

CHAPTER 8

LEAD THROUGH GRACE AND GENEROSITY OF SPIRIT

*Wisdom strengtheneth the wise more than ten
mighty men which are in the city.*

—ECCLESIASTES 7:19

Mary Magdalene found wisdom by turning inward and focusing her mind on God. In the Gospel of Mary, we learn that Jesus praised her for understanding better than the other disciples and promised to reveal to her the mysteries of Heaven. Reading this gospel, we can see that Mary Magdalene used not only her mind, but also her intuitive understanding. Mind is critical to our reasoning ability; we reason through all the appropriate information before making important decisions. Wisdom, on the other hand, comes through knowledge of truth, right and just judgment, discernment, and insight. Men call these feelings that fall outside of linear, logical thought "gut instinct," but women call such responses "intuition" or "sixth sense."

When Andrew and Peter doubted both the veracity and validity of Mary Magdalene's secret teaching, she deflected their hostile energy and shifted the conversation to Jesus' words and teachings. It's a mark of good leadership to be able to defuse volatile situations and get everyone back on track. In many ways, Mary Magdalene appeared to be both a graceful and wise leader.

Perhaps you have known or worked with a supervisor or manager who acts like a demagogue. People like this may take credit for employees' hard work, create drama with a knee-jerk management style, move from one crisis to the next, or make every meeting all about them. Such personalities are not limited to secular jobs, however; they may also be found in church leadership positions as well. An old adage states that when you are full of yourself, there is no room the Lord.

Mary Magdalene epitomized the antithesis of a demagogue. Though endowed with the full range of human emotion, she exhibited great strength of character and moral fiber in a time of crisis (specifically, during Jesus' torture and death). In her dealings with chauvinistic men in the Hebrew society of her time, she revealed a maturity and generosity of spirit that is worthy of emulation, not only by the average spiritual seeker, but also by leaders of companies, corporations, and countries.

Powerful Women, Gentle Warriors

Women do not have to become like men to have indomitable spirits and strong wills. True, there have been women, even modern women, who have sounded war's battle cry: England's Margaret Thatcher, India's Indira Gandhi, and Israel's Golda Meir, among them. They were women of character, disciplined and highly focused—traits often associated with the aggressive masculine warrior.

But there have also been many fine exemplars of the gentle feminine warrior. Mother Teresa of Calcutta made her mission caring for the poorest of the poor, and no one could stop her. When she needed money, she yoked her will to God's and asked people to find charity within their hearts and to be generous. If it meant she had to get on an airplane, even in poor health, and fly around the world to ask for funds personally, she did. Diana, Princess of Wales, used her power, grace, beauty, and compassion in working to rid the world of land mines and to change world governments' conventional thinking about using such weapons. Oprah Winfrey speaks to millions about love, forgiveness, and the power of transformation during segments of her television talk show. Incest, spousal abuse, personal empowerment—there is almost no subject from which she shies away. Searching for ways to overcome the negatives in their lives, Oprah and her guests offer messages of hope and meaning that resonate with a large viewing audience. Hilary Rodham Clinton, the former first lady currently serving in the U.S. Senate—a male-dominated political bastion—wrote a book about the need for a village. In doing so, she reminded us all that it takes parents, clergy, community members, business people, and others working together to raise healthy, happy, safe, and well-adjusted children. Like their ancient sisters, many modern women are imaginative and visionary. Though perhaps ridiculed by men, they can envision a world without hunger, poverty, and war.

Men see the world quite differently. They fight for principles, believing in war if it is the "right" course for a particular situation. But Jesus was unlike most men: Jesus was King of Peace. Perhaps that is why Mary Magdalene and so many other women were attracted to Him and His message.

Regardless of how compelling the argument, mothers do not like to see children they have conceived, carried for nine months inside their bodies, birthed, and raised go off and risk their lives on lonely, violent battlefields. Mothers found in Jesus someone who loved His male followers but had a soft spot in His heart for women and children.

Mary Magdalene, as Jesus' friend and constant companion, would have noticed how He empathized with the plight of the so-called "weaker sex." What woman wouldn't find that endearing? She saw how Jesus aligned His will with God's will, and she would have emulated His example in every way possible. She watched Him, the leader she most admired, work God's miracles upon the poor, the hungry, the sick, and even the dead. She watched Him and learned.

According to a French legend, Mary performed her first miracle for the barren wife of the prince of Marseille. The couple had practiced ritual sacrifice to idols hoping for the boon of a child, but Mary told them to stop. Later, in a vision, she told them that if they would stop persecuting Christians, she would ask God to allow them to conceive. Mary Magdalene didn't say she would grant their wish, only that she would ask God. More important, when the miracle occurred, she gave all glory and honor to God. She didn't go about gossiping to her friends and promoting herself to others as a healer. She didn't seek adulation for possessing the gift of healing. She credited God and retained her humility. But everyone would have known that through her own blessedness, she had blessed others.

FAST FACTS : Six Rules of Christian Conduct

Peter the apostle reminded those in the Christian communities of Asia Minor to stick to their beliefs despite the threat of persecution and death. In the First Letter of Peter in the Bible, he reminds the faithful (thought to be mostly Gentiles) about the six rules of conduct. (I Peter 3:8–9) These guidelines are as relevant for leaders today, both male and female, spiritual and secular, as they were during Mary Magdalene and Peter's lifetimes.

1. **Be of one mind.** One mind means that all are united with one will, one purpose, and one vision.
2. **Show sympathy to others.** Be generous in giving aid to others. Develop a kind heart. Be tender when dealing with those who are suffering the travails of life.
3. **Love one another.** This is one of Jesus' primary teachings. He said for us to love one another as He has loved us.
4. **Render compassion.** When others suffer hardship and sickness, reach out with compassion. Do what you can to lighten their loads.
5. **Be humble.** Cultivate humility. No one likes being around an arrogant, self-serving person. Remember the saying about pride: It goeth before a fall.
6. **Respond to evil acts against you with blessings.** Jesus said to turn the other cheek when someone smites you. We have to learn to curb the natural tendency within us to strike back.

Mary's Words Have Modern Resonance

When you read the Gospel of Mary, you begin to question why, until recently, we have only known about gospels named after men. Why have the only examples of disciples and apostles known to us been men? And why have only men become priests, bishops, cardinals, and popes in the Catholic Church? Feminine leadership and feminine symbols certainly existed in the early Christian Gnostic communities. Are we now to believe that the image of God is only a male image? Or that men's words are more sacred than women's words?

The records of Mary's own words in the Gospel of Mary, the Gospel of Philip, and the Pistis Sophia reveal Mary Magdalene to be an insightful and eloquent questioner of Jesus. She didn't query Him to upstage others present, but rather to fill in the blanks of her own knowledge and understanding. In the Pistis Sophia, Mary gazed at nothing for a time, perhaps digesting Jesus' information and forming new questions in her mind. Instead of interrupting Jesus or the other disciples, she held back and then asked Jesus to command her to speak openly. When she did speak, Peter complained about her to Jesus, saying that because she got in the way and talked all the time, none of the men could speak. But Jesus basically responded to Peter's complaint by saying something akin to the modern phrase, "No one is stopping you from asking." Mary Magdalene, filled with the spirit of light, stepped forward and explained her understanding of Jesus' teaching. Jesus was pleased, assured her that she had got it right, and praised her.

Now, we are learning that Mary Magdalene was speaking openly to Jesus, asking Him questions, explaining her interpretation and understanding, and getting it right. This fact raises a controversial modern question. Did Peter (who, in some writings, shows hostility toward her) and Paul and others conspire against Mary Magdalene, keeping secret the fact that she and all subsequent generations of spiritual women had God-given equal power and spiritual authority? Did God plan for men and women to work independent of one another or together as equals? In the modern Church, neither scenario represents current convention.

Have you ever experienced anything similar to the situation between Mary Magdalene and Peter? Has someone (a coworker, colleague, or so-called friend) ever seemed intent on taking you down a notch just because he or she feels threatened? Was this person confrontational, questioning what you had to say, devaluing your words, and effectively silencing you as though your words didn't matter? Helping women claim their voices and take their rightful place in the world is at the heart of the feminist movement. Eve did not fear to speak the truth to God. Neither did Mary. Why should we?

Love As Free-Flowing, Sacred Energy

If love is something sacred that we receive from God and can express to our dear ones, why do we not think to send it to our enemies as well? If we can ask for our own highest good, why can't we ask for the same blessings of goodness on those toward whom we feel enmity? Why bother, you might ask. Because doing so shifts the energy. Love isn't something that should be doled out in a parsimonious way or based in a deep-seated selfish desire. We ought to give love freely to all, whether they seek it or not, and without any expectation of a reward. Love can be offered as a silent blessing when we pass someone in the subway, the grocery store, at the bank, in school, or during a meeting. Even if you don't believe it has any effect, try it and notice the change inside yourself.

As a contemplative, Mary Magdalene spent many hours in worship, that is, in silence, prayer, and meditation. As her heart expressed love, it established a kind of magnetic pull to God. God, Who is light, Who initiated light and separated it from darkness, and Who made the light of the world become flesh to dwell among us, must have filled Mary Magdalene with His love and also His light. By cultivating an interior life, we too can receive God's holy light and love.

MEDITATION FOR TURNING INWARD

Wear loose clothing. Sit in a comfortable chair, spine erect and both feet on the floor, your open palms in your lap. Close your eyes. Put your inward focus on an imaginary point centered between your eyebrows. Take three deep cleansing breaths. Release all the tension your body may be holding. While gazing inward, put your mind's focus on the base of your spine. As you breath in, feel warm energy moving up the spine to the center of your crown. At the crown, the energy turns. Feel it become cool as it moves with your outgoing breath back down to the base of your spine. Repeat the cycle. Do this seven times. Then breathe naturally. Sink into the silence. Feel the peace it offers. Give yourself an autosuggestion to dive deeper next time.

Follow Mary's Example of Female Discipleship

What kind of example does Mary Magdalene reflect to us across the centuries? First, we know that Mary Magdalene so aligned herself with her teacher Jesus that she mirrored His teaching for all time. Who was her model for discipleship? It was certainly not another disciple, neither male nor female, who was around Jesus at the time. No, her model for perfect discipleship was none other than Jesus Himself, Who submitted His will to God the Father, to whom He gave all glory and honor. Jesus declared that He was the way, the truth, and the light.

Then spake Jesus again unto them, saying, I am the light of the world: he that followeth me shall not walk in darkness, but shall have the light of life.

—JOHN 8:12

Mirroring Jesus, Mary Magdalene would have also been full of light. She would have stood up for truth and been openly courageous (as she was when she stood at the cross in support of Jesus). If challenged about her beliefs and spiritual ideals, could she have done less than speak up and speak out as Jesus had? When Peter was hostile to her during her questioning of Jesus, Mary Magdalene showed that believers have to be brave enough to speak up, even in an atmosphere of animosity. Unlike the other disciples, Mary Magdalene must have so closely identified with Jesus that, in essence, part of her was united with Him. Unlike Peter, who denied Jesus three times before the cock crowed, she did not deny Him even once. Did she ask Jesus for a chief position in His kingdom once it was established, as James and John did? No. Did she doubt Jesus like Thomas, who needed to put his fingers in the risen Jesus' wounds in order to believe? No.

Mary Magdalene was obedient, faithful, courageous, certain, committed, and accountable to Jesus and none other. She comprehended Him and His truth more than all the others, and she knew and accepted the requirements for being a disciple—repentance, belief, faith, commitment, love and hunger for God, and a desire to serve humanity. How do we emulate her example? By first venturing into that inner realm of the unknown, charting our own darkness, and acknowledging the holes in our wholeness we will be able to embrace the light. Only then, armed with knowledge of the flip side of light, can we serve as light bearers for the dark places in the world.

Make Your Questions Count

Idle chatter gets us nowhere, but thoughtful questions can unlock important meaning, furthering our understanding of a particular subject. Spiritual questions can be asked in the open or in devotional silence. Mary Magdalene, we learn from reading the translations of the Gnostic texts and the scholarly commentaries on them, was apparently quite bright and understood the spiritual significance of many of Jesus' statements. But that did not stop her from questioning Him.

Think well before speaking. Then decisively ask your question or make a statement. Don't back down from asking difficult questions. But do ask yourself whether it is necessary to be confrontational. Is there, instead, a graceful way to ask this question in order to elicit a meaningful response?

THE MEANING OF BLESSING

A blessing means a benefit, a gift, mercy, or a special favor. There are myriad mentions of blessings in both the Old Testament and New Testament. In her anointing of Jesus, Mary Magdalene was blessing Him.

When we feel down, a quick way to pick ourselves up is to count our blessings. In the Old Testament, God offered many blessings to His children. The New Testament is replete with instances of blessings. We bless God when we praise Him and express our love and gratitude.

Dive deeply into the silence following prayer and seek answers to your most burning questions from an inner source. The Catholic Church teaches that the Holy Spirit leads believers in the many paths to prayer and is also the anointer that permeates a person's whole being. In silence, beckoning this power can cause myriad questions to bubble up from your inner well of inquiry. Not only questions come, but the answers you seek may emerge as well. Who knows what blessings may come?

Learn to Live an Inner-Directed Life in the World

Never give up your right to think for yourself. Others are only too eager to think for you. We all have our individual pathways that lead us on an inward journey. We can't be content to find all our knowledge outside ourselves or get it from other sources. How dependable are those sources? How are we to glimpse the truth and experience grace if we are not willing to dive inward and drink from our inner well of wisdom?

Ways to Invoke the Holy Blessings of Saint Mary Magdalene

Make a sanctuary in your garden. Use mosaic stepping-stones, statuary, bird feeders, and plants that attract butterflies. Sit in a warm, safe place and invoke Mary Magdalene, praying for light and love. Listen to the birds, feel the touch of the breeze, smell the scent of herbs and flowers, and behind the sheets of your eyelids, enter the darkness and ask for light.

Transform a plain wooden box, a garden jug, or an urn with a lid. Any of these can become a sacred vessel to hold your messages to Mary Magdalene. If using a box, decorate it magnificently with holy images, exotic or handmade paper, pretty ribbon, beads, and scriptural verses written in gold or silver pen. If using a jug or urn, cover it with beautiful mosaic art fashioned out of broken bits of pottery, beads, buttons, marbles, sea glass, and small religious objects glued on with mastic and grouted with gray or some other neutral color. Or paint the jug with pottery paint and write sacred verses around it. Whenever inspiration moves you, jot down prayers, messages, poems, meditation insights, and thank-you notes to Mary Magdalene concerning your spiritual life, your hopes and dreams, and your career or work—in short, anything about your life as a spiritual woman. Keep them in your sacred box or urn.

Affirmations

≈ *I will reflect each day on the feminine face of God.*

≈ *I will study the lives of my sacred sisters who lead through grace and generosity of spirit so that I may become more like them.*

There are those who say we are cocreators with God and that our world is created from the inside out by our thinking and our choices (both conscious and unconscious). If you wish to lead through grace and generosity of spirit, you must be willing to open yourself to the greater power guiding your life.

✳ THE MEANING OF WORSHIP

The act of worship means to venerate or pay homage to God. This expression of reverence can be done with or without rituals and rites. In practice, those who worship show love, veneration, and adoration without asking for anything in return. Worship does not necessarily involve prayers of thanksgiving. Instead, it is the communion of the soul with God.

Saints and mystics had busy lives and, in many ways, difficult lives. Try chopping wood, carrying water, catching the chickens, plucking and cooking them, washing the clothes by hand, making the cheese—you get the idea—and still finding time for prayers and meditation. What's our excuse?

An excellent book to read that will inspire you and get you thinking about women's wisdom from many different spiritual paths is *Sacred Voices, Essential Women's Wisdom through the Ages*, compiled and edited by Mary Ford-Grabowsky. In this collection of stories, you will read how ancient and modern women have discovered paths that led them into various journeys, as documented by their own words.

Make some prayer blankets for the sick. At certain churches, women make these simple security blankets throughout the year for those battling disease. The blankets are constructed from two yards of material—one yard each for the front and back. Choose suitable material in spiritual, healing colors and patterns, avoiding wild color combinations and garish images. The material must be washed and prayed over before you begin cutting. In addition, every stitch must be prayed over to infuse the blanket with love and healing prayers. Praying over every stitch is not difficult even when you use a sewing machine. Listening to spiritual music, even singing along, counts as prayer.

Listen to the composition by Samuel Barber titled Adagio for Strings. Sometimes music can draw us more deeply into ourselves than anything else. The beginning of this composition is moody and hauntingly beautiful with its low and mid-tone notes. As the melody begins to climb higher, close your eyes and imagined that your very soul is being lifted and carried to its source. Allow your mind to embrace the idea of mystical union with the Christ, as Christian mystics and Catholic saints have done for centuries.

Affirmations

I will hold high the lamp of truth to illuminate the snares and pitfalls of ignorance.

Be an Advocate for Women Who Desire to Serve

An advocate is someone who defends or intercedes on behalf of another. We know Mary Magdalene emulated Jesus, who, as we also know, was a great advocate. Even more, He was positively radical in His egalitarian treatment of women and men. While Christianity in its earliest era was trying to find its moorings, women served as preachers, teachers, and witnesses to the word of God. Women were important, as already noted, to Jesus' ministry. As wives, sisters, disciples, martyrs, missionaries, prophets, and consecrated widows (and, in later times, heads of orders), women would have served as advocates for one another.

It is possible that while they were serving in roles that previously were forbidden to them, misogyny did not just disappear. A woman like Mary Magdalene could stand as a shining example to other women and have men tolerate her, but she could not change their view about women in general. Men of that period might have argued that Jesus made it possible for her to transcend her femaleness. But they would have been missing the point entirely: Her femaleness was precisely the source of her inner strength, intuition, and knowledge.

Scholars believe there may have been a deliberate effort by the canonical gospel writers to de-emphasize Mary Magdalene. But what if the responsibility of carrying Jesus' ministry forward had been placed on Mary Magdalene and the women instead of on the men? What do you think would have happened? Would Christianity have remained viable, spread around the world, and endured attacks on it from many forces and directions? Would women have remained advocates for one another or become adversarial?

Does playing the blame game level the playing field?

We'll never know the answers for all of these "what ifs," but one thing is certain: We have to work from where we are now. Modern women who hunger for knowledge like their ancient sisters Mary Magdalene and Eve are fighting the same uphill battle for secular and sacred authority. They desire to be exemplars, to share their wisdom, to unite their flocks, and to steer a steady course toward God. But there are still people opposed to this idea.

Some men, like their first century counterparts, still judge righteousness by gender rather than by mind and behavior. There are still those orthodox believers who follow a literal translation of the Bible, believing that women are innately inferior and must submit to the will of their husbands. Only when women become the gatekeepers for the highest levels of corporations and churches is it likely that a level playing field will ever exist. To get there, be an advocate for women who desire to serve.

Prayer to Saint Mary Magdalene

MY SISTER MARY MAGDALENE, my holy light, pray for me that I may grow strong in spirit and in grace. May I live an exemplary life, serve others, and become a courageous advocate for just and right causes. Help me be wise enough to understand the role of spiritual womanhood. Inspire me to seek the feminine face of God as embodied by you and other female saints who entered the sacred bridal chamber. Inspire me to be ever conscious that within my heart and soul, I radiate the beauty of the Divine. As I traverse my inner and outer worlds, fill me with the conviction that you—the fountainhead of countless women through the ages—walk alongside me, leading me along holy paths of righteousness and comforting me when I feel afraid. Help me to remember that behind all existence is the hand of our Creator. Saint Mary Magdalene, may I become emboldened, confident, courageous, and inwardly directed to always follow your example of holy love—inviolable and ever constant—for Jesus. Amen.

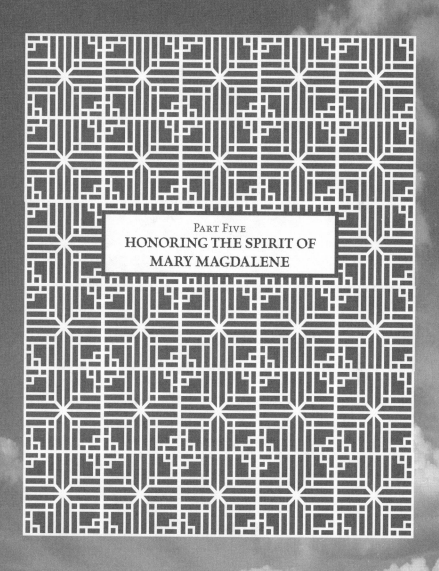

PART FIVE
HONORING THE SPIRIT OF MARY MAGDALENE

CHAPTER 9

BRINGING THE GOODNESS AND BLESSINGS OF MARY MAGDALENE INTO YOUR LIFE

*Mary said, "Tell me Lord, why I have come to this place to profit or to forfeit.
The Lord said, "You make it clear the abundance of the revealer."*
—THE DIALOGUE OF THE SAVIOR III: 60–61,
THE NAG HAMMADI LIBRARY

Have you ever wondered what God's plan is for your life? Maybe you have an inner sense of what you are meant to accomplish. Many of us aren't too sure. Yet, if we spend just a little time thinking about our calling, identifying what we feel most passionate about, and deciding how we could translate that passion into our life's work, we might discover the higher power that's blowing wind into our sails.

Tapping into our spiritual core empowers and magnifies our work. Practitioners of Karma Yoga say that, because all glory and honor belongs to God, we must work at our tasks with love and attention and not be attached to the fruit of the work. But when we feel passionate about what we do, it empowers us to do our best. Our products or services are enhanced by the energy of love flowing through us as we work.

How, then, do you know if you are moving on the right course for your life? One way is to use that very question as a point of departure into meditation. Jesus said, "Ask, believing, and ye shall receive." Expect an answer, even if it isn't the one you want.

It is clear from the question Mary Magdalene asked in the previously quoted conversation with the Savior that she not only thought about her life's purpose but also understood that she could either gain or lose. Why else would she have asked that question? Perhaps she thought that through her intentions and actions she might gain in wisdom, understanding, and love. Or perhaps she wondered if she would receive an outpouring of visions and dreams through God's grace. And what would she lose (or have to give up)? Some of us might be thinking about that ourselves. What must we forsake in order to follow a spiritual path in alignment with our life's purpose? What good things might come to us if we do?

Jesus validated that Mary was aligned with her purpose, for He told her that she made clear for others the abundance (or fullness) of meaning in His teachings. How beautiful is that? Mary demonstrated a remarkable ability to comprehend the complexity and nuance of His parables and discourses. Further, she easily communicated her understanding to others. Because of that, her teacher validated her. Perhaps that is why it was so easy for the early Gnostic Christians to revere her as the embodiment of Sophia (Divine Wisdom).

*. . . incline thine ear unto wisdom, and apply thine heart to understanding;
Yea, if thou criest after knowledge, and liftest up thy voice for understanding; If thou seekest her as silver, and searchest for her as for hid treasures;
Then shalt thou understand the fear of the Lord, and find the knowledge
of God.*

—PROVERBS 2: 2–5

In modern language, we'd call Mary Magdalene a self-actualized woman. Her spiritual ancestresses were the Jewish women who made all the preparations for the Sabbath on Friday evening and lit the candles that brought light into the home. They represented the spiritual epicenter of the family, and they inspired all good endeavors, just as they do today. The Talmud says, "It is a woman alone through whom God's blessings are vouchsafed to a house." To be a bearer of God's blessings, truth, and goodness and to inspire others to action—these sacred duties certainly found expression in Mary Magdalene's life.

They can find expression in ours too, if we can just remember that with God, we are cocreators of our lives. If your life isn't working for you, get help and figure out why. Is it the company you keep? A job you hate? The lack of any meaningful purpose or direction? Are you living a life out of balance—too much work, too little play, with no time for spiritual endeavors? What do you really want to do, and with whom? What are the old habits or patterns of behavior that you need to change? Figure out the "baby steps" you must take to shift direction and change course. No one is going to do it for you.

Invite the Embodiment of Wisdom into Your Life

If you are like so many of us, you have a great longing inside. There are myriad ways we try to fill our longing. We seek out companions, friends, and lovers. We marry or don't. We may grow apart from our partners and become divorced or widowed. In some cases, we marry again. We think that if we can just find that special someone with whom we feel safe, protected, and loved, we'll be complete and the great longing inside us will subside. But even when we do find that one "right" person, it does not absolve us from the responsibility of continuing to work on ourselves in order to fulfill our life and make it complete. It's our responsibility and no one else's. The Talmud says that each of us is a creature of God and each has a calling. One person's accomplishments might be large while another's are small, but the rewards for both are the same if their hearts are set upon Heaven.

Mary Magdalene absolutely had set her heart upon Heaven. In life, she found Jesus, but death physically separated them. Did Mary Magdalene feel that deep longing tugging at her soul after Jesus' death? He was obscured from her eyes, but not her heart. When He said her name, Mary, she recognized Him and called out Rabboni (Master). She must have been reassured about the continuity of the human spirit when she saw His transcendent form after He had risen from the dead. But when she could not embrace Him and was forced to realize that she would never again touch His earthly body, it must have been a torturous moment.

Still, she had a life to live and a purpose. She stayed the course, continuing Jesus' ministry. She took responsibility for her own life and its direction. Perhaps she became a contemplative so she could commune with Jesus in an interior space, thereby appeasing her soul's longing for Him. But she didn't just give up, throw away her body, and end her life. And, as far as anyone knows, she didn't spend the rest of her life complaining about her fate. On the contrary, with determination, she faced adversity and change, perfected her spiritual practices, and strengthened her resolve to love God ever more deeply.

By night on my bed I sought him whom my soul loveth: I sought him, but I found him not.

I will rise now, and go about the city in the streets, and in the broad ways I will seek him whom my soul loveth: I sought him, but I found him not.

The watchmen that go about the city found me: to whom I said, Saw ye him whom my soul loveth?

It was but a little that I passed from them, but I found him whom my soul loveth: I held him, and would not let him go . . . .

—SONG OF SOLOMON 3:1–4

Somewhere between the outer world and the inner world of the soul is a threshold, and it exists in each one of us. It invites us to enter into a process of discovery. At some point, Mary Magdalene surely felt her soul's longing for contact with the Divine. She chose to cross the threshold and make her way back to the source of her being. By turning inward, she found fulfillment. Many saints of different religions have spoken of the ecstasy of that mystical union. Labyrinth walkers say that through the walking, there is always a process of discovery about oneself. There are so many tools available to people today to find their way into living a

FAST FACTS : The Scriptural Teaching about Immortality

How can we understand the complex concept of immortality? The Bible explains it in different ways. Here are a few:

Deathlessness and incorruptibility together define immortality. Humans were made in God's image, and God is immortal; therefore humans were created with immortality as part of God's plan. Death does not and cannot destroy the human soul.

And fear not them which kill the body, but are not able to kill the soul: but rather fear him which is able to destroy both soul and body in hell. —MATTHEW 10:28

Adam and Eve sinned in the Garden of Eden, but their souls' immortality was not lost as a result of their sin. The wage of sin is death (physically). Humans die, but their souls continue after death.

Wherefore, as by one man sin entered into the world, and death by sin; and so death passed upon all men, for that all have sinned. For until the law, sin was in the world: but sin is not imputed when there is no law. —ROMANS 5:12–14

Redemption is through belief in Jesus Christ. Yet nowhere is it written that unbelievers will be annihilated. Each person is judged by his or her actions in life. The Catholic Church has one last stop for sinners called Purgatory. For those who die with sins unabsolved, prayers may be said for their salvation and special works of penance, almsgiving, and indulgences may be performed on their behalf.

For God so loved the world, that he gave his only begotten Son, that whosoever believeth in him should not perish, but have everlasting life. —JOHN 3:16

At death, the soul survives separation of body and soul. The body decays, but the soul continues on its journey to its final, eternal resting place.

We must all appear before the judgment seat of Christ; that every one may receive the things done in his body, according to that he hath done, whether it be good or bad. —II CORINTHIANS 5:10

The soul dwells in a state after death for a period of purging before it can enter Heaven, according to the Catholic Church's teaching.

Then said Jesus again unto them, I go my way, and ye shall seek me, and shall die in your sins: wither I go, ye cannot come. Then said the Jews, Will he kill himself? Because he saith, Wither I go, ye cannot come. And he said unto them, Ye are from beneath; I am from above: ye are of this world; I am not of this world. I said therefore unto you, that ye shall die of your sins: for if ye believe not that I am he, ye shall die in your sins. —JOHN 8:21–24 meaningful life, tapping into Divine wisdom, and honoring the spirit of Mary Magdalene.

When we, like Mary Magdalene, turn our attention away from the senses and the world in order to turn inward, we too can discover our destiny and find inner truth. We sense an awesome and immense presence within us. Here we find the safety, security, and love we have been searching for outside ourselves. It becomes clear pretty quickly that it is not our relationships in the world that nourish us as much as regular contact with the long-hidden and suppressed parts of our souls.

According to the Kabbalah and Jewish mystic tradition, every soul is a scintillating spark of the Divine. Perhaps it is easier for some to conceptualize an amalgam of sparks as the image of God rather than an omnipotent, omnipresent, and omniscient masculine entity that excludes any trace of the feminine. Since we've been told that we are made in God's image, does that mean that God has both masculine and feminine qualities? For many women, the face of the bride is every bit as important as the face of the bridegroom. By inviting the embodiment of wisdom into your life, you now have a holy feminine face to gaze upon. It's a face that Jesus loved. Ask Mary Magdalene, bride of Christ (at least in the mystical sense), to help you move your life in a spiritual direction and keep it on course. Invoke her. She will come.

Walk in wisdom toward them that are without . . . .
—COLOSSIANS 4:5

Surround Yourself with Sacred Imagery

In some ways, what our eyes see dominates our lives. Make this work to your spiritual advantage. What images make you feel holy? Perhaps stained-glass windows, gardens in bloom, crucifixes, sunsets, religious paintings, holy cards, candles decorated with saints' images and prayers, illustrated manuscript pages, and iconographic patterns stir up feelings of reverence and devotion within you. Or maybe it is an ancient vessel, something you can envision holding sacred papyri fragments much like the vessels that once held the Dead Sea Scrolls or the Gnostic gospels. Is your response to such images strong or weak? Maybe for you sacred imagery is an inspirational book about angels. Or perhaps it's a framed image you bought on vacation in France that shows a Black Madonna partially obscured behind iron fretwork and jugs of calla lilies. Or does that little bottle of anointing oil invite you into the sacred silence?

Regardless of which specific things resonate within you, sacred imagery should call you to the inner journey. Discover what turns you toward that ancient echo calling you within. If you are feeling lost and alone, adrift without direction, spiritually barren, and living a life that you feel has no worth, consider that someone else is only too aware of your plight.

Are not five sparrows sold for two farthings, and not one of them is forgotten before God? But even the very hairs on your head are all numbered. Fear not therefore: ye are of more value than many sparrows.

—LUKE 12:6–7

Sacred imagery can help us replace spiritual avoidance with action. You don't need an altar, although some people find them important. Five or ten minutes a day is sufficient to establish a habit of prayer and meditation. Without cutting into sleep, how much time could you carve out of each day? If only five or ten minutes, fine. But it often takes most people that long just to wind down and release the stress. Still, it's a start. You have nothing to lose and untold blessings to gain.

But thou, when thou prayest, enter into thy closet, and when thou has shut thy door, pray to thy Father which is in secret; and thy Father, which seeth in secret, shall reward thee' openly.

—MATTHEW 6:6

Open Yourself to the Gifts of Spirit

Read the many sources listed at the end of this book and decide for yourself who you believe Mary Magdalene was—devoted disciple, loving confidante, wife of Jesus, apostle, heir apparent, or Sophia, goddess of wisdom. As you grow in knowledge of her, you might find your life being profoundly blessed and enriched. As you begin to turn inward in prayer, meditation, and contemplation with Mary Magdalene as the focus, you might notice meaningful signs and symbols as well as images in dreams and meditations. Learn to use them as deciphering tools.

You might feel energy coursing through you. Your steps might become metaphorically and physically lighter on the planet. Your intuition might get stronger, along with your ability to discern between ordinary conversations and words of wisdom. Once you tap into your inner resources, silence becomes an enjoyable escape from the noisy chaos of life.

But even the silence is not silent. As you dive deeper into meditation, you will begin to hear subtle sounds that sometimes become more audible. You might even see flashes of light. Your sense of self might expand to feel as large as the sky or as small as an insect. These wondrous things are markings along the road of an inward journey. When you are no longer attached to your body in the same way, death holds no fear for you because you "die daily," in the words of the apostle Paul. You taste freedom. You experience the wisdom of love as unselfish love for others, much like God's love for all His creatures. Such love encircles you, but never confines, imprisons, or possesses.

 ## HEALING WITH SAINT MARY MAGDALENE

What follows is a guided healing meditation. It's best done with a partner or another spiritual seeker. Since meditation and prayer go hand in hand, ask your partner to say the prayer with you. Then, while you close your eyes and relax, allow him or her to read the guided imagery part. Energy follows thought, and the body accepts what the mind tells it. You are creating a positive environment for healing to take place.

Instruction: Light a candle and recite the prayer that follows. Find a comfortable place to sit or lie flat on your back on the floor (on a yoga mat or blanket) with your hands out to the sides, palms up. Make sure you have a blanket for warmth (a prayer blanket would be perfect: see Chapter 8).

Take three deep breaths, releasing all tension in your body. Close your eyes and focus them upward between your eyebrows (do not strain). Have someone read the following words as you listen to the reading and imagine the images.

Prayer: *Hail Saint Mary Magdalene, strengthened by Jesus' love and empowered by the Holy Spirit with the gift of healing, look graciously upon me in my hour of need. I am in the battle for my life and desperately need your help. Holy Mother Mary Magdalene, I implore you to use your powerful intercession to Jesus, the unblemished Lamb of God, in bond with the Holy Spirit to bring upon my body now the healing it needs. I am clearing my mind and opening my heart to receive the wondrous gift of healing. Amen.*

Meditation: Imagine that you are in a safe place and that the sun is shining upon you. It warms your body. Take a deep breath in. Imagine your body is a porous membrane that light can easily move through. Breathe in the light. The healing warmth penetrates every bone, muscle, ligament, organ, tissue, and cell. Your body is now bathed in healing light. Be present with this feeling in your mind. Let it become familiar.

Now let your mind focus on the area of your body most in need of healing. See that diseased area as dark. Breathe in the light of perfection; breathe out the darkness of imperfection. Let the darkness, the illness, the disease, go. Breathe in; breathe out. As the dark cells leave your body when you breathe out, they coalesce together and become a black ball. Breathe in the light. Breathe out the dark, allowing your breath to push the dark ball out to the horizon where it disappears. Repeat the process as many times as necessary to eliminate all the darkness. Imagine light filling that part of your body where the dark dwelled. See every cell in that area bathed in warm, healing light. Know that the light is restoring perfection to each cell. Breathe naturally for as long as you can, just allowing the perfection to be restored. Think about this statement:

The vision of God is perfect. The mind of God sees perfection. God sees you as perfect and whole. Be healed. Be whole. Believe, and give thanks.

Bring Mary Magdalene into Your Life

Mary Magdalene would have experienced the unselfish and merciful love of God as one who was a conduit for that love. It must have nourished her soul and nurtured her body. How else could she have survived on a holy Eucharist wafer once a day and lived to be over seventy, as an old French legend claims?

Equally important, love's sacred energy would have flowed through her eyes, heart, and sweet smile to others. Stories in many cultures of the world tell of holy men and women whose touch could heal, whose mere presence transformed hearts and minds, and whose blessings poured forth without petitions or fanfare on those around them and even those far away. Such is the power of sacred, unselfish love.

If we repeat Mary Magdalene's stories and legends as well as share her wisdom, holy words, and loving kindness with others, we are rescuing this saint from the margins of the Bible and restoring her to her rightful place in the mainstream. She is as close as your breath. Whisper a prayer to beckon her. Seek her counsel, wisdom, and blessings for your life.

Therefore we ought to give the more earnest heed to the things which we have heard, lest at any time we should let them slip.

—Hebrews 2:1

Expand Your Network and Build a Spiritual Community

On the other side of silence, we move out into the world and meet other women like us who are also searching. Women seem to have an innate knack for networking. Around the country they are bringing about a revival of interest in Mary Magdalene that is unrivaled except perhaps in the Middle Ages and the first century. Women are teaching each other, sharing their wisdom and experiences, and supporting one another in their spiritual practices. Women are re-enacting ancient rites and establishing new rituals to mark special moments on their sacred journeys. As if turning over a coin, some women are replacing the punishing masculine face of God with a loving, nurturing, sacred feminine face.

While some are faithful to the churches of their childhood, other women are also forming their own churches. They are the gatekeepers and priestesses in new faith communities that allow them to be leaders and caretakers of their flocks. These women have learned how to be servants of the work. They find that when their purpose is clear, the work almost seems to know what needs to be done. That experience can be both joyful and humbling.

There are many ways you can begin to build a center of spiritual sisterhood. It begins with one or two individuals interested in a deeper exploration of their religious beliefs. Build on each other's passions. One woman's passion may lead her to learn to read Greek so she can better understand the Scriptures and ascertain just how much patristic layering happened in translations over the centuries. Another woman might feel strongly about facilitating discussion and debate, while yet another's strength is in leading prayer. Someone else might enjoy cooking something for the group. Do you see how you could all come together and share your gifts? Each group establishes its own rites and rituals (often, these grow out of inspiration as the group grows closer, feels safer, and is guided by the word of God). Maybe one group closes with a prayer circle while another re-enacts something akin to the Last Supper.

Besides discussion groups, prayer circles, and spiritual meditation groups, retreats with a focus on Mary Magdalene have been springing up around the country. (Refer to the section on retreats in Chapter 7 for specific Web sites to help you find those focused on Mary Magdalene.) Speakers may include feminists, theologians, historical scholars, and followers of Mary Magdalene. For all the orthodox and Gnostic churches established in Mary Magdalene's honor, there are other less official groups studying this mysterious woman's life.

Ways to Invoke the Holy Blessings of Saint Mary Magdalene

Sew a simple, miniature picture quilt. First find an image of Mary Magdalene that you like and have it copied onto a fabric square. Use that square as the center of your quilt. Place other quilt pieces in lovely colors and interesting patterns around the square (your focal piece) until you have a pleasing rectangular design. Sew the pieces together and add padding (optional), a back, and edging. Hand-sew a two-inch wide piece of fabric across the top back side of the quilt so you can slip a dowel through. Tie a length of ribbon onto the dowel at each end. Hang your Mary Magdalene quilt and enjoy.

Mix a batch of lavender soap. Craft stores carry soap-making kits. Follow the directions for making the soap. Add fragrant French lavender oil in remembrance of Mary Magdalene's time in France. Write a note about Mary Magdalene and then wrap the soaps in pretty paper. Seal them with tape or a wax stamp, tie the note around the bar with pretty ribbon, and give them as gifts.

Create a box shrine for your desk or altar. A cigar box or a cardboard or wooden craft box works best. Find a beautiful image of Mary Magdalene and reduce it, if necessary, to fit into

Affirmations

> *I affirm that there are many paths to God, and I will respect the religious traditions and spiritual longings of each person I meet on the road to the Divine.*

> *I aspire to become pure and holy like Saint Mary Magdalene, radiating light, love, and peace to all.*

the top half of one side of the box. First, line the box by gluing and pasting in old pages from hymnals or missals that have been aged and/or distressed. Glue in the picture of Mary Magdalene. Make a frame by gluing seed pearls or sparkling colored beads around the paper image. You can paste a small framed copy of a prayer to Mary Magdalene, either below the picture or on the opposite side. Add other items that remind you of her, such as a cross, a miniature plastic or wooden unguent jar, a skull, and rose petals. Place miniature candles and holders inside, to be taken out and lit when you desire to honor her.

Make some rose perfume. Mix together ¼ cup of rose water, 1 tablespoon of rosemary oil, 2 tablespoons of rose oil, 1 tablespoon of storax oil, and 1 cup of undenatured alcohol or vodka. Pour this over rose petals in a screw-top jelly jar and seal with a lid. Keep sealed for three to four weeks while the perfume cures. Shake it to mix the scents and, after one month, pour it through a strainer into smaller bottles or pretty atomizers. Do this in honor of Mary Magdalene.

Affirmations

❧ *I will invoke Mary Magdalene to sanctify my prayer with her grace and love before I offer it to the Lord.*

MARY MAGDALENE WEB SITES

The Internet offers an abundance of information about Mary Magdalene. To get started, just type her name into Google or another search engine, or enter one or more of the URLs listed below.

www.Magdalene.org: This site offers a distinctly Gnostic view of Mary Magdalene, as well as recommended books.

http://newadvent.org: This Catholic site offers a more orthodox view of Mary Magdalene. The site has its own search engine, so type in Magdalene and it will bring up pages about her.

http://members.tripod.com/~Ramon_K_Jusino/magdalene.html: Here, from research done by America's foremost Catholic scholar, Raymond E. Brown, you'll find a forceful argument based on Gnostic Christian writings and the Johannine Community to support Mary Magdalene's being the author of the fourth gospel.

www.catholic.org: This Catholic site offers a concise hagiography of Mary Magdalene.

www.FutureChurch.org: FutureChurch is a national coalition of parish-centered Catholics who seek the full participation of all baptized Catholics in the life of the Church. The site offers an informative, in-depth text about Mary Magdalene.

What Blesses One, Blesses All

Throughout this book, you have found prayers and other ways to venerate the goodness and blessings of Mary Magdalene. Since this book has nine chapters, you may use each of the end-of-chapter prayers collectively as a novena to Mary Magdalene. Just say one prayer each day for nine days. Add your petitions or simply say the prayers in honor of her. Use your prayers, your special novenas, and the goodness that flows to you from Mary Magdalene for the good of people around you, not only family and friends, but also total strangers. There's an old adage about finding a penny. It only brings good fortune when you give it away. Think of blessings like that. A blessing shared blesses you even more.

Reach out for connections to others. Let your blessings extend out into your community. Adopt six or seven projects that help others throughout the year. Let your spirituality be reflected through service. Blanket, food, and book drives can supply the poor with an extra layer of warmth, can feed the hungry, and can get knowledge into the hands of those who can least afford it.

Instead of hosting the Thanksgiving or Christmas celebratory dinner at your house, offer to work as a server in a soup kitchen. Do fundraising for a homeless family to get them a house. Contact Habitat for Humanity to see what role you can play in manifesting this great gift for another. If swinging a hammer is your thing, by all means volunteer your services. Clean out closets and cupboards once a year and donate discarded clothing and food to shelters for battered women and children. Give of yourself and your time. Be a Big Brother or Big Sister. Volunteer at a local hospital.

Emulate Mary Magdalene's example of love, and remember that prayer itself is an act of love. Dive deeply within in silence, and on the other side of silence, give unselfishly in the world.

Prayer to Saint Mary Magdalene

SWEET SAINT MARY MAGDALENE, I have sent out my soul call to the Lord. While I wait for Him to join me in the temple of silence, will you, dear Saint Mary Magdalene, guide me in the preparation. I will cast off my old ways of thinking. I will throw out negative emotion. I will polish those recesses and corners of my soul-mind that have become blackened by wrong thought, word, and deed. I will prepare for the infusion of light and wisdom with your help and intercession. Holy Saint, inspire me to read and meditate on the secret teaching that Jesus gave you about the soul passing through seven realms to ascend to its eternal resting place. Show me how to merge my individual light into the light of the Divine. Guide me in purifying my soul so as to attract the light of the Holiest of Holies. Amen.

THREE SPIRITUAL PERSPECTIVES
ON MARY MAGDALENE

A Christian Perspective:
An Interview with Reverend Dr. George C. Fitzgerald

Dr. George C. Fitzgerald, S.T.D., director of the Spiritual Care Service at Stanford University Medical Center in Palo Alto, California, offers a Christian perspective of Mary Magdalene. His voice and soothing manner fit perfectly with his role of spiritual healer, someone who brings solace to the medical center's patients and their families in their time of need.

Prior to working at Stanford, Dr. Fitzgerald served as director of Pastoral Care at Princeton Medical Center and at San Francisco's Pacific Presbyterian Medical Center. Also an author, seminar leader, consultant, and member of many professional associations, he shares his insights on various aspects of Mary Magdalene's life and leadership, as well as their implications for modern women.

Based on his work ministering to others, Dr. Fitzgerald is in an excellent position to address the question of whether or not our world is experiencing a spiritual hunger. "From the longer perspective of world history, I would say no," he responds to this question. "Even in the preChristian times, it appears that a *sense of the spiritual* saturated the community. If we shift the focus to the last 150 years," he observes, the answer is, "yes, we are experiencing a greater spiritual hunger, as the promises of industrial and scientific progress have failed to deliver the goods—in terms of giving a sense of meaning and direction to life. Within my own realm of providing spiritual care in a university medical center, the transition within the last thirty to thirty-five years has been almost revolutionary."

In the past, Dr. Fitzgerald explains, the medical community virtually ignored books about spirituality and healing; however, within the last ten years or so, "books are pouring off the presses, and doctors are reading and discussing them. The difference is that almost every one of these authors has M.D. after his or her name, and most have been trained in our top medical centers."

When asked about what accounted for all the present interest in Mary Magdalene and what the nature of her relationship with Jesus was, he responds, "I suspect the main impetus for the increased interest in Mary Magdalene has come from women—in churches, universities, and seminaries—who are seeking feminine models of faith. There aren't too many in the New Testament. I am inclined to believe that her relation with Jesus was much like that of the other disciples. My sense is that her place for the followers of the way, for the first two generations after the death of Jesus, was comparable to that of the other disciples."

Why, if she was held in high esteem in the early church, did her reputation become tarnished?

Dr. Fitzgerald answers: "As they [the apostles and their followers] dispersed to the East and the West, Mary Magdalene was overwhelmed and devalued by the patriarchy that dominated the existing cultures, whether in Rome, Asia Minor, or India. In essence, she was defamed and demoted."

So why did it take the Church so long to correct the defamation of Mary Magdalene's reputation?

"I do not really know the particulars," explains Dr. Fitzgerald, "but I suspect they [leaders of the Catholic Church] were overwhelmed by biblical scholarship; and they have some of the best. In addition, [today] women appear to be taken a bit more seriously—as they become scholars, administrators of orders and facilities such as medical centers. Of course, there will be no ordination of women under the current pope. But I suspect one day the ordination of women will be accepted in that tradition."

Mary Magdalene revered Jesus, her teacher, but is it possible there was something more to their relationship—could they have shared a romantic or marital intimacy? Dr. Fitzgerald believes most Christians do not think an intimate relationship existed between Jesus and Mary Magdalene. "If substantive evidence were produced that proved the case, that would not be a problem from my faith perspective," he explains, but adds, "I am more inclined to believe that Jesus and Mary Magdalene would have married, if such a relationship existed. I cannot help but feel that Jesus would have been aware that such a situation would have quickly destroyed Mary Magdalene's reputation."

When asked whether Mary Magdalene went with Saint John, the Evangelist, to Ephesus after Jesus' death or to southern France where there are abundant legends about her, Dr. Fitzgerald offers no idea or opinion but asserts that "it is quite likely that Mary Magdalene, like the other disciples, left Palestine after the death of Jesus. As I recall, persecution intensified in Palestine, and the disciples also felt a strong compulsion to spread the wonderful news and newness of life they were experiencing—even in the face of death," he says.

"Women today can draw inspiration and spiritual meaning from Mary Magdalene's life and her relationship with Jesus and the other disciples by just accepting the fact that she was part of the inner circle of disciples,"

Dr. Fitzgerald adds. "That is tremendously meaningful for many women of faith. It should also enrich the faith of men as well."

Ask any woman who wants to serve why she can't get into the highest echelons of leadership within the churches of the world, and she is likely to point to a stained-glass ceiling. When questioned about whether he thought that Jesus, through His example of inclusion, was showing the world a way of bringing women into the inner circles of our churches, Dr. Fitzgerald says, "Today, in most mainstream Protestant denominations, women can occupy all levels of leadership, although they [churches] still are reluctant to choose a woman over a man for their priest, pastor, or rector. So the transition is still very much in process. I think Jesus would be quite happy to have a woman bishop or pope," Dr. Fitzgerald suggests, but "many fundamentalists still exclude women from leadership positions as well as ordination. Still," he continues, women "can use Mary Magdalene as an example to feel more comfortable and justified in seeking ordination and seminary and university teaching positions, as well as leadership posts within their denominations."

While some people perhaps would agree that women feel their spirituality deeply and are more at ease than men in expressing it, the centuries-old practice prevails of passing over women and choosing men as spiritual leaders. Yet spiritual hunger is palpable in our world that once, according to Dr. Fitzgerald, did not have that hunger as it does today. He notes, "Plutarch, in the first century C.E.[A.D.], said, 'If we traverse the world, it is possible to find cities without walls, without letters, without wealth, without coin, without schools and theatres; but a city without a temple or practices without worship, prayers, and the like, no one has ever seen.'"

That was a time when *the sense of the spiritual* saturated the community. By emulating Mary Magdalene in her deep devotion to Jesus, perhaps modern women can initiate a shift, serve those who are spiritually hungry, and establish again that *sense of the spiritual within our communities.*

A Gnostic Perspective:
An Interview with Rosamonde Miller

This interview with Rosamonde Miller, hierophant, spiritual successor to Mary Magdalene, and founder of the Church of Gnosis (Ecclesia Gnostica Mysteriorum), took place at a busy coffee shop next to Kepler's bookstore in Palo Alto, California, a mile or so from the Stanford University campus. Rosamonde (her name means "rose of the world") spoke of what she likes to call "a quasi nomadic" background originating in Carcassone, France—the area in the south of France that is so rich with stories and legends of Mary Magdalene, the Black Madonnas, the Knights Templar, Merovingian kings, and the Crusaders. Her title of hierophant, or initiator, is similar to that of bishop in the Catholic Church.

Rosamonde Miller is a free spirit who agrees with recent neuroscientific research that the human brain is, in fact, hardwired for mystical experience. She describes her work—*wild gnosis*—as approximately meaning "knowing through direct, transforming experience, left untamed and unconditioned by cultural and socioreligious beliefs: the state prior to the interpretation of the experience, uncaged by concepts and images."

Speaking perfect English with a lovely French accent, she explains that she lived in several countries while growing up. She says she loves science, history, and languages—she speaks several. Middle-aged, she is quite beautiful in a sensuous, womanly way. A thick mass of wavy auburn hair brushes past her shoulders and frames her face and delicate features. Her intense hazel eyes, softly lined in a mauve pencil, cast a direct, intent gaze. Her finely chiseled cheekbones and full, unpainted lips resemble a pre-Raphaelite model. You can't help but wonder if Mary Magdalene might have looked like her.

Gesticulating often to express a point, Rosamonde speaks with increasing animation. "The spirit of each of us is enlightened from our birth, and that's what Mary Magdalene represented," she says. Because of many different factors, we, as children, soon forget what great knowledge we possess, she explains, and we lose the openness that lets us know how to perceive it. All too soon we close down, but the ability—the knowledge—it's still there.

"There are no particular rituals or actions we do or courses of study we undertake that can give us what we always had," she continues, "but many of those things may help us awaken and bring to consciousness what has already been there. The *gnosis* is as close as our own heartbeat. It's our spirit that knows and experiences that sense of the extraordinary, numinous 'Presence.' When Jesus answered a question from Mary Magdalene in the Dialogue of the Savior, saying, 'Because you reveal the greatness of the Revealer, the living God dwells in you and you in Him,' this is what He was referring to," Rosamonde explains. But we get so caught up in our society and in culture's dogma and the labels put upon us and everything else, she says, that our view narrows. "We no longer see with our spirit as an expansive lens."

She pauses to sip her water, and when she continues, it's to discuss the connection between life and breath. Saying the word *breath* in several languages leads her into the topic of the Bible's first book, Genesis. Rosamonde says that she loves the motifs of dark and light at the beginning of the two creation myths in the book of Genesis. "All begins with the breath, and it is with the breath—that first breath—that once the body has been made and complete, that flesh becomes a living soul."

Her insights about the breath and about dark and light motifs are fascinating. Her openness makes it easy to ask her what she thinks about the current speculation by some that Mary Magdalene and Jesus were married.

"It is very unlikely that Jesus and Mary Magdalene married," she says emphatically. "Neither would have wanted that. In those days, marriage was all about ownership. The tales about Mary Magdalene and Jesus having a child are just stories," she explains, adding, "There's something in our brains that needs stories, archetypes, and myths. As long as we don't take them literally and confuse them with history, we can remain conscious and benefit by them."

Rosamonde explains that she was not aware gnosis was such an integral part of her until she experienced its absence. When she was nineteen and living in Cuba, Fidel Castro's secret police seized her as a political prisoner and beat, tortured, and repeatedly raped her during interrogation. Up until that point, she had devoted her life to God and had even considered entering a convent. At the hands of her captors, however, joy, light, and that sense of the Presence that she had always experienced left her. She descended into a state of darkness and hopelessness. One day, she heard a conversation between the officer in charge and a cohort. His conversation was animated because he was about to give a puppy to his little daughter. Realizing that even the monster who had authorized her torture had a loving side, Rosamonde experienced a powerful insight into the nature of humanity. That intense understanding was something she felt "to the marrow of her bones," an insight that "left her trembling with her teeth chattering." She says it was then that she understood humanity, "not as a set of opposites, but as a whole fabric, woven of light and dark threads, and we (that man and myself) were all part of it."

In that defining moment—overwhelmed with gratitude and filled with compassion—she began to pray for all sentient beings. The Presence again filled her, bringing peace and healing to her soul. After she was taken to a hospital and her injuries treated, a Catholic priest talked to her and offered to help her escape. She was flown to Spain and later to Paris, where priestesses from the Holy Order of Mary Magdalene met her and escorted her to their secret place in the south of France. They shared with her their works as well as their Gnostic material, and they subsequently initiated and appointed her near the day of her twentieth birthday.

Listening to Rosamonde speaking about her experiences, it was easy for my thoughts to drift back to Mary Magdalene and imagine how she too might have spoken, enjoining her listeners to look within.

A Roman Catholic Perspective:
An Interview with Christine Schenk

Sister Christine Schenk, a nun in the Congregation of Saint Joseph in Cleveland, Ohio, serves as executive director of FutureChurch, a national coalition of parish-based Catholics working to effect change in the Catholic Church. She has a master's degree with distinction in theology from St. Mary's Graduate School of Theology, a bachelor of science in nursing, magna cum laude, from Georgetown University, and a master's degree in nursing from Boston College.

Through a vigorous public speaking and writing program along with postings on FutureChurch's Web site, www.FutureChurch.org, Sister Schenk educates Catholics about issues related to "women in the ministry, optional celibacy, inclusive language, and Church decision-making that involves all the faithful, as called for by Vatican II." She oversees the organization's Web site, which provides a newsletter, posts thought-provoking articles, and offers projects as well as links to other related sites. Controversial discussion topics on the site include Corpus Christi, the campaign for optional celibacy; the future of the priestly ministry; the celebrating of women witnesses (women leaders and saints were not passive and deferential to their male counterparts as they have long been portrayed); women in church leadership; and Saint Mary of Magdala. In addition, she created and administers three national dialogue projects—Women in Church Leadership, The Future of Priestly Ministry, and Celebrating Women Witnesses. Sister Schenk wrote a brochure about Saint Mary of Magdala that she estimates has been distributed to more than 50,000 people. In it, she debunks much of the misinformation and misconceptions surrounding the life and reputation of the Bible's other Mary.

When asked who the historical Mary of Magdala was, Sister Schenk says she believes "Mary of Magdala was Jesus' disciple-confidante and friend. There is no biblical or historical evidence to support the notion that Jesus and Mary of Magdala were married. Biblically, had she been married, Mary would have been described as Mary, the wife of Jesus. The notion that Jesus and Mary of Magdala were married derives from a medieval myth. There is no mention of their marriage in early Christian or biblical texts even after the fall of Jerusalem in A.D. 70, which would have removed any need to hide this fact because of threats from the prevailing religious political leadership of Israel, which was now defunct."

When asked in what ways Mary Magdalene might have been a leader and for whom, Sister Schenk asserts that "in all the synoptic accounts, Mary Magdalene is named first in the list of women leaders who accompany Jesus from Galilee to tomb . . . much as Peter is listed first in listings of the male disciples. Extra-canonical gospels (in particular, the Gospel of Mary) also portray her as a leader and teacher of the male disciples."

Although the Church reversed its position about Mary Magdalene being the repentant prostitute and corrected its missal, why does the Church still not officially include Mary Magdalene in the Easter Sunday liturgy?

Sister Schenk believes there is "still latent—if not blatant—sexism in lectionary selections and translations. The Easter Sunday and holy week liturgies seem to reinforce the notion that only men were the major players in the central mysteries of the Christian faith, when, in fact, the Gospels themselves paint a different picture. There, we see it was Jesus' female disciples who seemed to understand His 'suffering servant' mission the best.

They accompanied Him through arrest, crucifixion, death, burial, and resurrection, while the male disciples fled to Galilee.

"That women were named as first witnesses to the Resurrection is regarded by biblical scholars as strong proof of the historicity of the Resurrection accounts," explains Sister Schenk. "Had these been fabricated by overly zealous disciples, women would never have been portrayed as the first witnesses to the empty tomb in a culture that did not accept them as legitimate witnesses in the law courts. This could be one reason that John's gospel is at pains to show Peter and the beloved disciple in a 'race to the tomb,' so that two male witnesses could corroborate the women's story."

What about the Church's biblical scholarship, and why did it take so long to rectify Mary of Magdala's miscast reputation?

Sister Schenk says it was only after Pope Pius XII issued *Divino Aflante Spiritu* in the middle of the twentieth century that biblical scholars finally had the leeway to apply the scientific method to their studies. Prior to that time, Catholic biblical scholarship was almost nonexistent. She explains that the Church's "biblical scholarship before that time was basically geared to proving *what the Church had always taught.*" She suggests that "thereafter, there was a flowering of Catholic biblical scholarship that the Catholic Church at large is still trying to catch up with. I believe it was in 1969 that the Church said there was no evidence that Mary of Magdala was a prostitute. Given the timeline, this was pretty fast.

"What is more mysterious to me is why average Catholics didn't hear about [the Church's reversal of its position] until we, at FutureChurch, began to celebrate her as the 'Apostle to the Apostles' in 1997," she continues.

Sister Schenk points out that when her organization started to disseminate historically and scholarly accurate information, people didn't believe it. It took about four years for the project to catch on.

When asked how women who are mothers can teach their daughters to serve as leaders, emulating Saint Mary Magdalene, Sister Schenk offers the following advice: "I would encourage modern mothers to read our 'Mary of Magdala' and 'Celebrating Women Witnesses' essays (which are modeled on the original Mary of Magdala effort) about historical and contemporary women leaders who resisted unjust structures because of faith in Jesus. Moms have to educate themselves before they can educate their daughters *and* their sons. There are many wonderful books out now by feminist Catholic women.

"Moms should also join a faith-sharing group or a women-church group to be nurtured and supported by other feminist women of faith. I have been part of such a group for eight years, and we have worked our way through many wonderful theological and biblical works by feminist women believers. If we don't have these kinds of supports, it can be hard to stay Christian when so much of what we hear in church excludes our gender both in language and leadership.

"Jesus," she explains, "included and supported women and called them to leadership and discipleship. We don't hear that in church, though it is present both in our history and biblical tradition. If we don't find it in church, we must nourish each other until the institution repents of its sexism and makes amends."

Assuming that one day the Church eventually does eradicate sexism, what new roles would women like herself love to take on in the Church?

Sister Schenk observes, "Catholic women should be free to follow the ministerial calls given by the Holy Spirit. If they believe they are called to serve as priests, at the very least the Church has an obligation to listen to them and test their calls, just as they listen to and test the calls of men."

In what direction does she see the Church heading in its relationship with women?

Sister Schenk answers, "Like it or not, the Catholic Church will have to deal with the women leaders who are, in fact, holding it together." Referring to an article she wrote for the newsletter *Focus*, Sister Schenk cites a little known fact that shows how women and lay ministers are the glue helping to hold the Catholic Church together. "Worldwide, there are 783,000 women religious serving the Church's 1.07 billion Catholics, compared to 405,000 priests. Add the nuns to at least 1.5 million female lay ministers (catechists, missionaries, and members of secular institutes) and it becomes clear that Catholicism's ministerial crisis cannot be solved without expanding women's roles."

These figures illustrate a need and a compelling reason to expand women's roles, but how might the process be started?

Sister Schenk suggests that the next step is to "ordain Catholic women deacons. This would legitimize women's sacramental ministry in the Church. Most Catholic women ministers in the United States (conservatively, an estimated 82 percent of 65,000 lay pastoral ministers and chaplains) already have qualifications (and more) to be ordained deacons immediately. As deacons they can preach, baptize, and witness marriages. This constitutes a huge new pool of ministers who could be readily available to help meet the sacramental needs of a growing church," she asserts.

"In the Anglican Church, women first became deaconesses, then deacons, and then they were ordained to the priesthood. According to two experts on the subject, John Wijngaard and Phyllis Zagano, the Church had deacons before we had priests as we understand priests today." Sister Schenk further explains that the apostle "Paul described [the Christian woman] Phoebe as *diakonos*, the same word he applied to himself. The ordination rites for women deacons [among the early Christians] were the same as those for men deacons, and they were regarded as sacramental. The reluctance of the institutional Church to seriously consider ordaining women deacons is probably linked to this fact. However, the Vatican has not closed the door on this discussion. Indeed it cannot, without seriously damaging its credibility."

Just don't expect the Catholic Church to begin ordaining women priests right away. Sister Schenk points out that it "will require lengthy internal processing, a change of canon law, and revision of some recent, rather prominent proclamations. Opening the diaconate to women, on the other hand, does not require such a complicated process, nor is it ruled out by canon law, according to the Canon Law Society of America. It seems to be a doable, reasonable next step."

Her outlook remains hopeful, despite the Church's past resistance to even consider positions of leadership for women. "Petitioning for women deacons does not mean we should stop calling for open discussion of women's ordination to the priesthood," she asserts. "To the contrary, it could be one key to reopening the discussion in the worldwide Church."

THE SURRENDER PRAYER

*T*o emphasize a particular point during her interview, Rosamonde Miller mentioned a prayer and began reciting it with her eyes closed, as if calling it forth from a place deep inside her. The words of the prayer speak to an ancient, intense longing for light and the desire for the presence of the Holy One. It's not hard to imagine that Mary Magdalene could have prayed just such a prayer. As you read and reflect on this prayer, open yourself to receive the blessings it holds just for you.

The Surrender
by Rosamonde Miller

I have been apart and I have lost my way.
The archons have taken my vision.
At times I am filled with Thee,
but often I am blind to Thy Presence,
when all I see is this world of form.
My ignorance and blindness are all I have to offer,
But these I give to Thee, holding back nothing.
And in my hours of darkness,
when I am not even sure there is a Thou, hearing my call,
I still call to Thee with all my heart.
Hear the cry of my voice, clamoring from this desert,
for my soul is parched and my heart can barely stand this longing.

BIBLIOGRAPHY

The biblical texts quoted in this book are drawn from:

The Holy Bible: Old and New Testaments, self-pronouncing edition, conforming to the 1611 edition, commonly known as the Authorized or King James Version. Cleveland and New York: The World Publishing Company. (No copyright or publication date available.)

The New Testament of Our Lord and Saviour Jesus Christ. Translated from the original Greek, Dutch-English edition. New York: American Bible Society, 1869.

Additional, supporting sources are as follows:

Artress, Lauren. *Walking a Sacred Path, Rediscovering the Labyrinth as a Spiritual Tool*. New York: G. P. Putnam's Sons, Riverhead Books, 1995.

Baigent, Michael, Richard Leigh, and Henry Lincoln. *Holy Blood, Holy Grail*. New York: Bantam Doubleday Dell Publishing Group, Inc., 1983.

Barrows, Anita, and Joanna Macy. *Rilke's Book of Hours, Love Poems to God*. New York: Penguin Putnam, Inc., Riverhead Books, 1996.

Borysenko, Joan. *A Woman's Journey to God*. New York: Riverhead Books, 1999.

Brock, Ann Graham. *Mary Magdalene, The First Apostle: The Struggle for Authority*. Cambridge: Harvard University Press, 2003.

Compton-Hernandez, Maria. *The Catholic Mother's Resource Guide, A Resource Listing of Hints and Ideas for Practicing and Teaching the Faith*. Goleta, Calif.: Queenship Publishing Company, 2002.

Cousineau, Phil. *The Art of Pilgrimage: The Seekers Guide to Making Travel Sacred*. Berkeley: Conari Press, 1998.

Dues, Greg. *Catholic Customs and Traditions, a Popular Guide*. Mystic, Conn.: Twenty-Third Publications, 2000.

Farmer, David. *Oxford Dictionary of Saints*. Fourth edition. Oxford: Oxford University Press, 1997.

Fox, Matthew. *Illuminations of Hildegard of Bingen*. Rochester: Bear & Company, 2002.

Gaffney, Mark H. *Gnostic Secrets of the Naassenes, the Initiatory Teachings of the Last Supper*. Rochester, N.Y.: Inner Traditions, 2004.

Giles, Mary E. *The Feminist Mystic and Other Essays on Women and Spirituality*. New York: The Crossroad Publishing Company, 1982.

Hanegraaff, Hank, and Paul L. Maier. *The Da Vinci Code, Fact or Fiction?* Wheaton: Tyndale House Publishers, Inc., 2004.

Haskins, Susan. *Mary Magdalen, Myth and Metaphor.* New York: Berkeley Publishing Group, Riverhead Books, 1993.

Hertz, Joseph Herman. *A Book of Jewish Thoughts.* New York: Bloch Publishing Co., Inc., 1926.

Higgs, Liz Curtis. *Unveiling Mary Magdalene.* Colorado Springs, Colo.: Water Brook Press, Division of Random House, 2001.

King, Karen. *The Gospel of Mary of Magdala: Jesus and the First Woman Apostle.* Santa Rosa, Calif.: Polebridge Press, 2003.

Klein, Peter. *Catholic Source Book, a Comprehensive Collection of Information about the Catholic Church.* Dubuque: Harcourt Religion Publishers, 2000.

LeLoup, Jean-Yves. *The Gospel of Mary Magdalene.* Rochester, N.Y.: Inner Traditions International, 2002.

L'Engle, Madeleine. *Walking on Water, Reflections on Faith and Art.* Wheaton, Ill.: Harold Shaw Publishers, 1980.

Lockyer, Herbert. *All the Women of the Bible.* Grand Rapids, Mich.: Zondervan, 1967.

Markale, Jean. *The Church of Mary Magdalene, the Sacred Feminine and the Treasure of Rennes-le-Château.* Rochester, N.Y.: Inner Traditions International, 2004.

Meeks, Wayne A. *The First Urban Christians, the Social World of the Apostle Paul.* Second Edition. New Haven, Conn., and London: Yale University Press, 2003.

Meyer, Marvin. *The Gospel of Thomas: The Hidden Sayings of Jesus.* New York: HarperCollins Publishers, Inc., 1992.

Meyer, Marvin, with Esther A. De Boer. *The Gospels of Mary: The Secret*

Tradition of Mary Magdalene, the Companion of Jesus. New York: Harper Collins Publishers, Inc., 1994.

Murphy, Cullen. *The World According to Eve*. New York: Houghton Mifflin Company, 1998.

Pagels, Elaine. *Beyond Belief: The Secret Gospel of Thomas*. New York: Random House, 2003.

Pagels, Elaine. *The Gnostic Gospels*. New York: Random House, Vintage Books Edition, 1989.

Picknett, Lynn. *Mary Magdalene*. New York: Avalon Publishing Group, Inc., Carroll & Graff Publishers, 2003.

Picknett, Lynn, and Clive Prince. *The Templar Revelation, Secret Guardians of the True Identity of Christ*. New York: Simon and Schuster, 1998.

Robinson, James M., Ed. *The Nag Hammadi Library in English: The Definitive Translation of the Gnostic Scriptures Complete in One Volume*. New York: Harper Collins Publishers, 1990.

Starbird, Margaret. *Magdalene's Lost Legacy, Symbolic Numbers and the Sacred Union in Christianity*. Rochester, N.Y.: Bear & Company, 2003.

Starbird, Margaret. *The Feminine Face of Christianity*. Wheaton, Ill.: Godsfield Press, Quest Books, 2003.

Starbird, Margaret. *The Woman with the Alabaster Jar: Mary Magdalen and the Holy Grail*. Rochester, N.Y.: Bear & Company, 1993.

Thorold, Algar, translator. *The Dialogue of the Seraphic Virgin Catherine of Siena*. Rockford, Ill.: Tan Books and Publishers, Inc., 1974.

SOURCES QUOTED/
PERMISSIONS AND CREDITS

In addition to Biblical passages, the following works have been quoted in the text of this book:

Barrows, Anita, and Joanna R. Macy. *Rilke's Book of Hours: Love Poems to God*. New York: Berkeley Publishing Group, Riverhead Books, 1996, page 4. Copyright ©1996 by Anita Barrows and Joanna Macy. Used by permission of Riverhead Books, an imprint of Penguin Putnam Inc.

Hertz, Joseph Herma. *A Book of Jewish Thoughts*. New York: Bloch Publishing Co., Inc., 1926, page 11.

King, Karen. *The Gospel of Mary of Magdala: Jesus and the First Woman Apostle*. Santa Rosa: Polebridge Press, 2003, pages 15 and 189.

Pagels, Elaine. *Beyond Belief: The Secret Gospel of Thomas*. New York: Random House, 2003, page 60.

Robinson, James M., General Editor. *The Nag Hammadi Library in English*,

3rd, Completely Revised Edition. Quotations as submitted from pages 133, 136, 148, 252, and 297. Copyright © 1978, 1988 by E.J. Brill, Leiden, The Netherlands. Reprinted by permission of Harper Collins Publishers, Inc.

Starbird, Margaret. *Magdalene's Lost Legacy: Symbolic Numbers and the Sacred Union in Christianity*. Rochester, NY: Bear & Company, a division of Inner Traditions International, Rochester, VT 05767, 2003, page 125. *www.InnerTraditions.com*

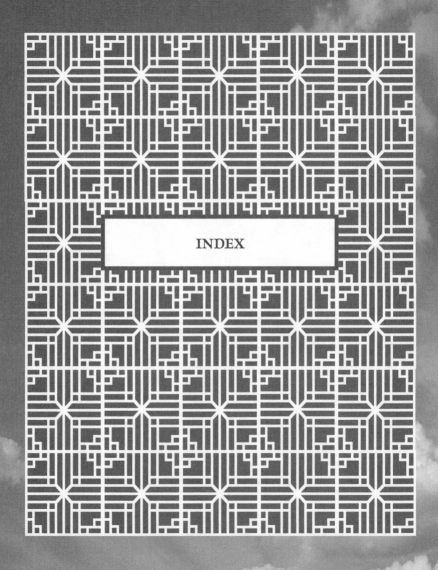

INDEX

A

Affirmations, 20, 21, 44, 62, 63, 78, 79, 98, 99, 132, 133, 154, 155, 170, 171, 194, 195
Almond, symbolism of, 75
Andrew, 72
Anointing, 58–60
Apostle, Mary as, 69–88
    Apostle to Apostles, 19, 70, 113, 118
    Beloved Disciple, 98, 104, 105, 106
    confidence of Jesus, 74–77
    following example of, 167–68
    inquisitive nature, 13, 16, 74, 164–65
    overview, 69–70
    role of women and, 70–71
    Thirteenth Apostle, 81–83
    See also Spiritual leadership (of Mary)
Apostles
    criteria for, 80–81
    marriage and, 86–87
    reaction to Mary's vision, 65–66
    summary of, 72–73
Arch, symbolism of, 120
Artistic portrayal, of Mary, 99, 108, 111–13

B

Bartholomew, 72
Beloved Disciple, Mary as, 98, 104, 105, 106
Beyond Belief, 105–6
Black Madonna, 122, 123–26
Blankets, making, 171
Blessings of Mary, 179–98
    Affirmations, 20, 21, 44, 62, 63, 78, 79, 98, 99, 132, 133, 154, 155, 170, 171, 194, 195
    bringing Mary into your life, 191–92
    building spiritual community and, 192–93
    general guidelines, 197–98
    healing meditation, 189–91
    inviting her wisdom in, 182–86
    prayers, 22, 45, 68, 89, 114, 135, 157, 175, 190, 199
    sacred imagery for, 187–88
    specific ways to invoke, 20–21, 44, 62–63, 78–79, 98–99, 132, 154, 170–71, 194–95
    See also Prayer; Spirituality, nurturing
Body, caring for, 149–50
Box shrine, 194–95

C

Canonical gospels, 102–3
Cathars, 33–36
Catholic Church. *See* Roman Catholic
    Church
Celibacy mandate, 133–34
Christians/Christianity
    early persecution of, 10–11, 100
    early power struggle, 96–100,
        101–2
    initial leadership, 12–13,
        107–9
    Mary's unifying influence, 17, 74,
        76
    modern perspective on Mary,
        202–6
    rules of conduct, 163
Circle, symbolism of, 121
Clement, Bishop of Rome, 11
Crusades, 36
Crystal chalice, 78

D

Da Vinci, Leonardo, 39–40
Daughter, of Mary, 119
Demons
    casting out your, 144–48
    Jesus casting out, 5
    seven, of Mary, 18
    struggling with, 3–4
Devotional walk, 44
Diptych altarpieces, 21
Discussion groups, 21
Dream journals, 62–63
Duke of Burgundy, 110–11

E

Egg icon, 66–67
Eve, Mary and, 127–30, 174

F

Femininity. *See* Women
Fig leaves, symbolism of, 75
Fish, symbolism of, 75
Fitzgerald, George C., 202–6
Forget-me-not flowers, 44
Forgiveness, 147–48
France
    Black Madonna and,
        123–26
    following of Mary in, 40
    Medieval reverence for Mary,
        110–11
    miracle legend in, 162
Frankincense, 20

G

Garden holy space, 132, 142–43, 170
Gelasius, Pope, 51
Gnostic Gospels, 15–17, 26, 27
Gnostics
  first-century, beliefs, 15–16
  a modern perspective, 206–9
  portrayal of Mary, 15–17, 81, 82, 107, 110, 118
  salvation according to, 86
  treasured texts of, 16–17
  view/treatment of women, 29–30, 54, 84, 85
God, connecting with. *See* Prayer; Spirituality, nurturing
Gospel of John, 41–43, 103–6, 107
Gospel of Luke, 107
Gospel of Mark, 107
Gospel of Mary, 15, 16, 17, 26, 28, 61, 164
Gospel of Matthew, 107
Gospel of Philip, 28
Gospel of Thomas, 15, 16
Grapevines/grapes, symbolism of, 75
Gregory I, Pope, 14, 27, 129

H

Healing meditation, 189–91
High priestess, 118
Holy Blood, Holy Grail, 4, 25, 31–33, 119, 120
Holy Grail, 31–36
Holy space, creating, 141–43
Holy Spirit, gifts of, 51–54
"Holy Tears" bottle, 154

I

Ignatius, Bishop of Antioch, 11
Immorality, scriptures on, 184–85
Inner-directed life, living, 169–72, 183–86
Inquisitiveness, of Mary, 13, 16, 74, 164–65
Intentions, establishing, 146
Isis connection, 124, 130–31

J

James the Elder, 72
James the Less, 72
Jesus
  healing Mary, 74
  hierarchy of authority and, 11, 80–81

as leadership model, 84

message of victory over death, 5

respect for Mary, 16, 17

in transcendent form, 5, 60, 74–75, 182

treatment of women, 9–10, 77–80, 84–85, 94–95, 162

Jesus/Mary relationship, 4–5, 18, 23–43

after Crucifixion, 115–19, 182–83

ambiguity/supposition of, 26–28

love and, 23–25, 74–75, 116–17

marriage questions, 29–31, 36–39, 86–88, 117, 122–23

Mary standing true, 93–94

Mary's vision/secret teaching, 61–66

modern texts on, 25, 31–33

New Testament Gospel speculation, 41–43

overview, 23–26

romantic speculation, 23–27

teacher/disciple, 26–27, 49–50. See also Apostle, Mary as; Spiritual leadership (of Mary)

John, brother of James the Elder, 73

John, Gospel of, 103–6

John Paul II, Pope, 19, 113

John the Theologian, 5

Judas Iscariot, 73

K

Kabbalah, 63

L

Last Supper, 39–40, 96

Lavender soap, 194

Lazarus, 7, 52, 126

Leadership. See Spiritual leadership (of Mary)

Lectio divina, 154

Life purpose

going inward for, 183–86

identifying, 179–80

Mary finding/living, 179, 180–81, 182–83

Lily, symbolism of, 121

Love

infusing, in everything, 140, 191–92

Jesus/Mary relationship, 23–25, 74–75, 116–17

as sacred energy, 165–66

M

Magdala (Migdal Nunya), 9

"Male" as divine, 16

Mandorla (seed shape), symbolism of, 121

Marriage questions, 29–31, 36–39, 86–88, 117, 122–23

Martha, sister of Lazarus, 7, 52, 126

Mary
in Aramaic, 17
as common biblical name, 6
confusion surrounding name, 6–9

Mary, mother of Jesus, 52

Mary, mother of John Mark (companion of Peter), 53

Mary, wife of Clopas, 6, 53

Mary Jacobi, 6, 53

Mary Magdalene
early life, 17–18
fact summary about, 8
later life, 95
legends/speculation about, 17–19
other Marys confused with, 6–9
world of, 9–11
See also specific topics

Mary of Bethany, 6, 7–9, 14, 19

Masks, of Mary, 62

Matthew, 73

Mazes, 121, 132

Medieval reverence, 110–11

Meditation, 166, 180, 188–91

Merovingians, 32–33

Miller, Rosamonde, 206–9, 217, 218

Miracles, of Mary, 162

Music, devotional, 154, 171

Myrrh, 20

N

Nag Hammadi treasures, 16–17

National Gallery of Art, 99, 108

Nature, nurturing power of, 155

Navette, making, 132

New Testament Gospel(s), 27
first Gospel, 107
Mary diminished in, 94–95, 107–10
Mary possibly writing, 103–6
writing/translation of, 109
See also specific Gospels

O

Olive trees, symbolism of, 76

P

Paintings, of Mary, 99, 108

Palm fronds, symbolism of, 76

Paul, 101

Peter. *See* Simon Peter

Philip, 73

Picture quilt, 194
Pistis Sophia, 15, 66, 81, 164
Poster, of Mary, 78–79
Prayer
    for healing meditation, 190
    Lectio divina and, 154
    meditation and, 166, 180,
        188–91
    regularity of, 148
    room, sanctifying, 154
    to Saint Mary Magdalene, 22, 45,
        68, 89, 114, 135, 157, 175, 190,
        199
    The Surrender, 217–18
Priory of Sion, 119–23
Prostitute, Mary as
    evidence vs. accusations, 5, 10
    myth, serving church, 11–14
    myth origin, 14
    Vatican reversing position on,
        19

Q

Questions
    Mary's inquisitive nature, 13, 16,
        74, 164–65
    as meditation starting point, 180
    thoughtful, 168–69

R

Red egg legend, 66–67
Respect, of Mary, 54
Responsibility, of Mary, 56
Retreats, spiritual, 152, 156, 192
Roman Catholic Church
    hierarchy of authority, 11, 12
    modern perspective on Mary,
        210–15
    papal celibacy mandate, 133–34
Rose, symbolism of, 121
Rose garden, planting, 132
Rose perfume, making, 195
Royal bloodline, 118–19

S

Sacred Feminine, 39–40
Sacred imagery, 187–88
Sacred knowledge, seeking, 143–44
Salome, mother of John, 53
Sara-la-Kâli, Saint, 125, 126
Schenk, Christine, 210–15
Secret teaching (vision) of Mary,
    61–66
Self-discovery, 147
Service, advocating for, 173–74
Seven, as sacred number, 59, 61
Sexual union, 37, 123, 131–33

Shakti, 64–65
Simon Peter, 73
    after Crucifixion, 95–96
    denying Jesus, 93–94
    leadership succession of, 13, 107
    marriage status, 86–87
    Mary's vision and, 65
    relationship with Mary, 13, 16,
        26–27, 84, 107, 165
Simon the Cananean, 73
Siricius, Pope, 133–34
Sleep, getting adequate, 150–51
Soul
    powers of darkness and, 64
    rise of, 64–65
    as spark of Divine, 186
Spider webs, symbolism of, 121
Spiritual community, building,
    192–93
Spiritual leadership (of Mary), 49–67
    anointing and, 58–60
    earning, 54
    gifts of Holy Spirit and, 51–54
    grace/wisdom of, 159–60
    Mary's vision/secret teaching,
        61–66
    modern resonance of, 164–65
    overview, 49–50
    responsibility and, 56

self-determined nature of, 55
spiritual evolution and, 56–58
trustworthiness and, 55
women, priesthood and, 51–54
See also Apostle, Mary as
Spirituality, nurturing, 139–56
    bringing Mary into your life,
        191–92
    casting out demons, 144–48
    creating holy space, 141–43
    definitive steps for, 153
    developing good habits,
        149–51
    following discipleship example,
        167–68
    living inner-directed life, 169–72,
        183–86
    opening to gifts of spirit, 188–91
    overview, 139–40
    reclaiming connection with God,
        151–55
    retreats, 152, 156, 192
    seeking sacred knowledge, 143–44
    thoughtful questions, 168–69
    See also Blessings of Mary; Prayer
Symbolism
    in Gothic architecture, 120–21
    of numbers, 59, 61, 83
    sacred, in Mary's world, 75–76

T

Tarot cards, 126–27

Thaddeus, 73

The Da Vinci Code, 4, 25, 31–32, 39, 118, 119

The Gnostic Gospels, 20. *See also specific Gospels*

The Gospel of Mary of Magdala, Jesus and the First Woman, 84

The Surrender prayer, 217–18

The Templar Revelation, 4, 36

Thirteenth Apostle, 81–83. *See also* Apostle, Mary as

Thomas (Judas Thomas), 73

Timothy, 100

Trustworthiness, of Mary, 55

T-shirt, declaring faith, 98

Twelve, symbolism of, 83

V

Vesica piscis, 79

W

Web sites, 196

Widow, Mary as, 115–19

Wisdom chalice, 117–18

Women

advocating service for, 173–74

around Mary Magdalene, 52–53

early Christian power struggle, 96–100, 101–2

empowerment of, 75, 77–80, 82–83

equality of, 12, 33, 82, 84, 95

feminine warriors, 160–62

Gnostic view/treatment of, 29–30, 54, 84, 85

intuitive, feminine aspect, 145–46, 159

Jesus' treatment of, 9–10, 77–80, 84–85, 94–95, 162

in Jesus' world, 13, 70–71, 97

nurturing spirituality. *See* Blessings of Mary; Prayer; Spirituality, nurturing

priesthood and, 51–54

Sacred Feminine, 39–40

Worship, meaning of, 172